Rock Hudson Bi
Behind the Camera Lens and Untold Stories

James Raymon Gunn

CONTENTS

Chapter 1
Chapter 2
Chapter 3
Chapter 4
Chapter 5
Chapter 6
Chapter 7
Chapter 8
Chapter 9
Chapter 10
Chapter 11

Chapter 1

Paris. I'm not interested in hearing about Paris. It's quite cold there. I'm sick of going to the doctor. They don't know anything and are powerless to act. I am not going to fucking Paris!

Rock Hudson's health was deteriorating at an alarming rate in July 1985. Every morning, butler James Wright discovered his bed sheets wet with sweat. Rock's weight had decreased from 225 to 170 pounds. He was struggling to keep food down. His body was covered with itchy rashes that drove him insane. He began to miss appointments and toured the home and grounds in his jockey shorts.

Only four people in the world knew Rock had AIDS: his secretary, Mark Miller; George Nader, who lived with Miller; James Wright; and Dean Dittman, an actor friend to whom Rock had confided shortly after finding he had the disease. For a year, these four had watched helplessly as Rock deteriorated before their eyes, yet they insisted on working and maintaining the appearance that everything was well.

They persuaded him to return to Paris, where he had received injections of the experimental medication HPA 23 in 1984. The medicine was thought to block the AIDS virus, but it worked like insulin and had to be taken on a regular basis. The infection would reappear if the injections were not administered. The treatment appeared to have been successful when Rock left Paris. His blood was cultured, but no AIDS virus was discovered. Rock had assured his doctor, Dominique Dormont, that he would return in a few months, but nearly a year had passed and Rock had refused to return. "I don't want to hear about fucking Paris!" he replied when pals suggested it.

Instead, he appeared in nine episodes of Dynasty, and when Doris Day asked him to be the first guest on her Christian Broadcast Network show, Doris Day's Best Friends, Rock agreed. Mark Miller told Rock the night before he was to travel for Carmel, California, to tape the show, "I don't think you should go."

"Why not, I'm perfectly fine."

"You're not fine."

"What exactly do you mean?"

"You don't appear well. You should avoid being noticed in public. present will be a press conference, and reporters from all over will be present to capture your and Doris' reunion."

Rock waved his hand, a move he used to reject or silence someone. "Doris is relying on me." I'm not going to let her down."

Later, Mark called Rock's publicity representative, Dale Olson, who was to accompany him to Carmel. Mark requested Dale to talk Rock out of going. Dale stated that he would try. Dale arrived at the Castle with a limousine the next afternoon to pick up Rock. He discovered Rock dressed and packed, but sounded asleep on a wooden bench next to the door. "Rock, this is ridiculous," Dale muttered as he awoke him. I'm not sure what's wrong with you, but you appear ill. "I'm canceling...

Rock stood up. "Come on, come on. We're off!" He went with obvious pain to the limousine and grunted his way inside.

He slept the entire way to the airport and on the plane to Carmel. "It's not too late, we can cancel..." Dale continued repeating.

"No way. I promised Doris that I would do it, and that's all there is to it!"

Rock arrived late for the Pebble Beach reunion. He'd fallen asleep shortly after arriving at the Quail Lodge, and Dale had hoped he'd sleep through the press conference. But Rock awoke, hunted around desperately for his shaving supplies, found them, shaved, and returned just in time for the last five minutes.

"It was devastating," Doris Day remembers of his entrance into the room. I didn't exhibit my emotions, although it crushed my heart. I really wanted to get him out of there and ask him, "Why are you doing this?"

Later, when clips from the press conference were aired on television, Rock's hair appeared stringy and oily, and his clothes did not match. But he wrapped his arm around Doris and looked at her tenderly. "I was watching another film of yours," he explained softly, "and then I saw one of you with me." You know what the distinction was? In you."

"Really!" Doris said.

Rock stroked her face with his finger. They appeared at ease and Serena together, like a man and his beloved companion in their golden years. "We had a good life, didn't we?" he appeared to say as he stroked her face and peered into her eyes.

The following morning,Doris tried to persuade Rock not to tape the show the next morning. She served him scrambled eggs, croissants, cottage-fried potatoes, and coffee, and they relaxed in the sun on her home's terrace. Rock only picked at his supper, she noted. "I'm worried about you," she said. "I don't want you to do this show if you aren't prepared. "So, what's the point?"

"I'm gonna do the show," Rock declared.

"Will you please stop that! You're not required... "I want to."

Doris fixed her gaze on him. "You're not being honest with me."

"I've been sick with the flu." I lost a lot of weight and can't seem to get it back."

"Do you suffer from anorexia? "Do you believe you're fat and want to be skinny?" Doris later stated, "AIDS did not even occur to me."

Rock assured her that it was only the flu. She inquired as to what he was doing about it and what his buddies had to say about it. "I believe you require the services of another doctor." I believe you should seek a second viewpoint. "I believe you should take action."

"You really think I should?" Rock said.

"Yes.,,

"Okay, I will."

Doris and Rock drove out to Stone Pine Ranch to film Doris Day's Best Friends. "We didn't push at all," Doris explains. We let him move at his own pace and laughed like crazy, just like old times. I believe he had more laughs--we were virtually on the floor with laughter."

Rock was supposed to arrive on a rickety old bus, go around the grounds with Doris and her dog, and sit and remember. Rock went to his trailer to sleep whenever he could. On the second day of shooting, he was invited to remain for dinner with the production crew and Doris. "Oh, no," he exclaimed, "I have to catch a plane." I have a birthday celebration to attend."

"I knew he wasn't going to a birthday party," Doris explains. That was entirely his invention. I knew he wanted to go home and sleep as soon as I sat down." She was, of course, correct. Rock Hudson's final performance would be on television, and it seemed fitting, even fulfilling, that it would be with Doris Day.

Rock returned to the Castle more malnourished and frail than when he fled. He appeared to be clinging to life by a thread. Mark Miller was strong, saying he had purchased plane tickets for Rock and Dean

Dittman to fly to Paris in two days. He had made arrangements with Dr. Dormont for Rock to be treated. He gave Rock a letter from a friend, Bob Darcy, who also had AIDS and had been receiving HPA treatment in Paris for thirteen months. Bob Darcy said that he had gained weight, was swimming two miles each day, and felt powerful. Rock let out a sigh. "All right, I'll go... but not with Dean." "I'm going with Ron Channell." Mark chose Dean Dittman since he was familiar with Rock's condition and would know what to do in an emergency. He hadn't contemplated sending Rock with Marc Christian because the two had been estranged for quite some time. They were living different lives, while Christian continued to sleep in a separate bedroom at the Castle. When Rock indicated he'd go with Ron Channell, Mark claimed he'd cancel Dean and switch. Whatever it takes to get Rock back to Paris.

Ron Channell (pronounced like the designer's name, Chanel) was a personal trainer Rock recruited in 1983 to come to his house and work out with him. Ron was a tall, muscular, strapping young man with thick black hair who shared Rock's juvenile sense of humor. They became friends. Ron began visiting the Castle for an hour in the morning several times a week, then five times a week, and finally he was staying for lunch and most of the day. He and Rock rode their horses around, laughing and doing jigsaw puzzles. They worked out together, and Ron would say, "Come on, guy!"

Ron made it apparent to everyone in the home that he was straight and only wanted Rock's friendship. However, the staff observed Rock becoming increasingly enamored. "He would practically sit by the window and wait for Ron," recounts Mark Miller. "When he awoke, the first thing he asked was, 'Did Ron call?'" When is he going to stop by?' Everything Ron did was fantastic."

In 1984, Rock invited Ron to accompany him to Europe for seven weeks to attend the Deauville Film Festival and relax. Rock would continue to pay him as a physical therapist. Unbeknownst to Ron, Rock was on his way to Paris to receive HPA 23 injections from Dr. Dormont. The treatment required Rock to travel to Paris every other week and undergo three-hour morning infusions. Rock informed Ron that he had script conferences in the morning and that he would leave the hotel with his briefcase and take a cab to Percy Hospital.

Between weeks in Paris, Rock and Ron visited London, Rome, Barcelona, and St. Tropez, where they went Mediterranean sailing. It was Ron's first vacation to Europe, and Rock adored being his tour guide, taking him first class everywhere. Both Rock and Ron stated that they had never had a better trip.

When Rock invited Ron to abandon everything and return to Europe with him a year later, Ron leaped at the chance. He had everything packed and was ready to depart the next day.

James called from the Castle on Saturday. "Mr. Hudson is extremely frail; he can hardly walk." He hasn't eaten anything. "I don't think he'll be able to fly." Mark and George get into their car and begin driving back to Los Angeles.

At the Castle, James kept checking up on Rock, who was still sleeping. "Mr. Hudson," he explained, "we have to pack." James always addressed him as "Mr. Hudson." James was a likable guy, an endearing blend of wildness and formality. He dressed casually and occasionally wore nothing but a towel, but he never sat at the table with Rock; instead, he perched on a stool behind the cooking island and always addressed Rock by his surname. "Mr. Hudson liked it because it kept us at a distance, which is correct. "Acquaintance breeds contempt."

Rock looked at James, perplexed. "Pack? "What for?"

"You're leaving for Paris."

"Not at all. No, not today."

"Yes. Tonight."

"I require a suitcase." "I need to go out and buy a suitcase."

James was baffled. "He had all different kinds of suitcases upstairs."

The doorbell rang, and it was Ross Hunter and Jacque Mapes on the other end. Many of Hudson's most famous films, like Magnificent Obsession and Pillow Talk, were produced by Ross Hunter. Hunter and Mapes had been regular visitors to the Castle over the years. They stated they were going out to lunch with Rock, and James walked up to announce it. Rock had forgotten about the date, but he dressed and went downstairs anyway.

"I heard you're going on a trip tonight," Ross informed her.

"I'm going to Paris."

"No," James replied. "You're going to Geneva."

Rock informed Ross and Jacque that he needed to purchase luggage. They offered to drive him to the baggage store, but Rock refused, saying, "No, I'll drive." "I just bought a new Mercedes." They debated, but Rock was unmoved. He had just purchased a black

Mercedes 500 SEL sedan because he intended to go on "double dates" with Ron Channell, he informed Miller.

Rock, Ross Hunter, and Jacque Mapes climbed into the Mercedes, and as Rock drove out of the driveway, he slammed into the gate. He swore, laughed, and then walked down the street. "He was in no physical condition to drive," James claims.

Rock went straight back to bed after returning without having eaten lunch but with a new suitcase. At four o'clock, James went upstairs to his bedroom. "We have to pack, Mr. Hudson." You're lying there. "I'll come get your belongings."

"Can I get you anything?" James inquired as he packed two suitcases.

"No," Rock replied before falling back asleep.

Around 7 p.m., Mark and George arrived at the Castle. Marc Christian was the one who answered the door. "We're here to see Rock." Christian made a broad motion toward the stairs, as if to suggest, "Go on up." They discovered Rock naked, wandering aimlessly around his bedroom. His skeleton appearance astounded Mark and George. "He looked like a famine victim, with his skin all wrinkled and hanging in flaps." When they discovered he hadn't eaten anything all day, they began a chant for a chocolate milkshake. "James makes the world's best chocolate shakes!" A milkshake! "Let's get a milkshake!"

Rock was jolted into the shower by Mark and George. When James brought up the shakes, Rock emerged from the shower and fell on a chair. George assisted him in putting on his shirt and slacks, then pulled on his socks and shoes for him while sipping on his milk shake. "Praise be to whatever powers," George exclaims, "he finished the entire milkshake.""

They were in excruciating pain as they walked away from Rock. They had been trying to get Rock on this plane for a year, but now they were wondering if it was too late. Will he survive? He was unable to dress himself. Will he even make it through the flight? Mark felt compelled to turn around and bring him back, but he reasoned, "At the other end of the rainbow, there may be help." There is no assistance here."

Mark and George circled the airport until the jet took off and they were certain Rock had not been turned back. Then, sick to their stomachs, they began the three-hour drive back to Palm Desert.

That night, they did not make it to the desert. They had to make a halt north of Los Angeles before continuing on Sunday morning. When they arrived in Palm Desert, the machine had an urgent message from Ron Channell in Paris. Rock had refused to eat or drink anything during the eleven-hour flight, even water. There was no limousine at the Paris airport. So Ron was stranded with three suitcases and a wheelchair-bound Hollywood star. Ron had gotten Rock through customs and into the VIP lounge, grabbed a cab, and loaded the baggage and movie star into it. When they arrived at the Ritz, Rock had collapsed on the bed and was breathing unevenly. "What should I do!" On the machine, Ron said.

Mark called Gary Sugarman, Rock's doctor in Los Angeles, and then called Ron back. "Get Rock into the American Hospital as soon as possible, by limousine or taxi, I don't care." He also advised him to contact Dr. Dominique Dormont. Mark stated that he will renew his passport and take the following trip to Paris.

When doctors at the American Hospital examined Rock and noticed the scars from his heart bypass operation, they concluded he had cardiac problems and admitted him to the cardiology unit. Ron Channell was unaware of and unable to inform them about AIDS. Because Rock was critically dehydrated, they began intravenous feeding. In the meantime, Ron dialed Dr. Dormont's number and left four messages on his answering machine. The first suggested contacting Mr. Hudson at the Ritz. Come as soon as possible, urged the second. Come soon, said the third. Mr. Hudson is in the American Hospital, according to the fourth.

Dr. Sugarman in Los Angeles called Dr. Dormont that night. He requested that Dr. Dormont transfer Rock from the American Hospital to Percy. "It's not like that in France," Dr. Dormont replied. The ideal thing is for someone close to Rock to come to Paris, and we'll go to the American Hospital and talk to the doctors together."

Mark entered Rock's room and discovered him half-conscious. Through the blanket, Mark gripped Rock's foot. "I'm here," he announced. "We'll take care of everything." Mark burst into tears. "When I entered the room, I knew he was going to die," he later stated. I hoped he could turn things around before Paris, but when I saw him in that room, I knew."

Rock mused that he was delighted Mark was present. "I just got in," Mark explained, "I'm going to the hotel, and I'll see you later."

There were reporters and cameras crawling all over the Ritz Hotel that night. Ron Channell was preoccupied with something else. The night before, he had finally reached Dr. Dormont, who had informed him that Rock had AIDS. "How come Rock didn't tell me! "My God, why wouldn't he tell me?" he exclaimed, breaking down in sobs.

"He'd never tell anyone," Mark remarked. "He just wanted to live a normal life."

Ron Channell was worried for Rock and sick for himself. He and Rock had ridden around on horses and exchanged snacks. When Rock first met Ron Channell's family, he kissed them. What if the sickness was spread by saliva? Ron was concerned that the press would erroneously identify him as Rock's boyfriend, and that his own career would suffer as a result of his relationship with someone with AIDS. Mark arranged for Ron to go to New York the next morning on the Concorde. "How am I going to leave?" "I'm not interested in being photographed," Ron stated.

"Ron, this is not my first day in pictures," Mark explained. "I'll get you out of here without anyone knowing." Mark stated that he would have a limousine waiting for "Mr. Channell" at the hotel's front entrance at 9 a.m. He would take Ron down a back hall and through a service entrance at 7 a.m., where a taxi would be waiting. Ron would completely miss the press. The strategy worked.

When Mark arrived at the hospital on Wednesday, July 24, he discovered Rock significantly improved as a result of the IV feeding. The color had returned to his cheeks, and the deep lines appeared to have been smoothed. Mark began to compliment him on how great he looked, but Rock waved his hand and asked, "Where's Ron?"

"I booked him a seat on the Concorde to New York." He left almost two hours ago."

A curtain appeared to fall over Rock's face, erasing all indications of expression. His next remarks were flat. "It was two hours ago. Why?"

"When he found out you had...," Mark added, "he went to pieces, into total panic."

Rock completed the sentence. "There's a plague." He shifted his gaze away from Mark. "I knew it was going to happen. That if he found out, he'd abandon me."

"He was shaking with fright," Mark observed. "He cried for the majority of the night." I booked his flight and then got him out of the hotel using the standard procedure...

Rock's voice was desolate, but his face and eyes remained expressionless.

"Nothing. Not even a farewell."

"He wasn't thinking," Mark pointed out. "He couldn't do it." He's worried that the press would label him as your last lover. Which they will if they can find him."

Rock rolled onto his side and faced the wall, away from Mark. Mark approached the picture window and stood there, observing the apartment complex across the street. He wondered if cameras or telephoto lenses were pointing at him from behind the darkened windows. He instructed the private nurse, a young Irishwoman named Ann, to keep the curtains pulled far enough to obscure Rock's vision. She dashed over to draw the curtains.Mark and Yanou went to watch Rock together on Thursday, July 25. "Don't cry," Mark advised her, so Yanou explains, "I tried to make it fun."

They discovered Rock sitting up in a chair while the nurses were making his bed. "Hey, Yanou, it's great to see you," he said. "Isn't this hilarious? I'm back in my favorite city, Paris, and I'm in the hospital."

Later that morning, Yanou and Mark learnt that Percy Hospital's commanding officer had overturned his decision and informed Dr. Dormont that Rock may be admitted. It's unknown who stepped in to help Rock. Some say Nancy Reagan called Mitterrand, while others say the French defense minister made the choice. However, President Reagan had called Rock in the hospital the day before. Rock informed Miller, "I got a call from the President."

"Oh, what did he say?"'Hello,' he said. Nancy offers her best wishes.' 'Good,' I said. I'm sending Nancy my love.' Then Ronnie responded, `We're both not in the best condition. [Reagan suffered from colon cancer.] I'm hoping we'll both be better in a few days."

"It was like a script," Rock continued. We each delivered our lines flawlessly. "But why did he call?"

Dr. Dormont arrived at the hospital later that morning to visit Rock. When Rock recognized the doctor, his face brightened up. Dr. Dormont examined Rock, took blood, and was astounded by how weak and dehydrated he was. He was far too weak to benefit from HPA 23 injections.

At 11 a.m., a conference was held at the American Hospital to decide what would happen to Rock. Mark, Yanou, and Dr. Dormont were present, as were the cardiologist and hospital staff. Everyone was concerned about something different. Certain hospital employees wanted Rock gone as quickly as possible. They couldn't hide the fact that he had AIDS and informed Mark that if he didn't make an announcement about it, they would. Some staff members hoped that Rock could be relocated before the announcement so that the hospital would not be connected with AIDS patients.

Dr. Dormont, on the other hand, desired that Rock remain in place until he was stronger. Mark Miller desired that Rock receive the greatest possible care and that his life be extended. "We were bargaining, trying to get Rock whatever we could." Yanou informed the press that a statement will be issued at 2 p.m. and began drafting the release. The statement was only one paragraph long, but the group debated it for two hours before it was acceptable to all parties. I

Mark returned to Rock's room. "I'm sorry, Rock," he replied, "but we have to inform you that you have AIDS."

Rock gave Mark a dismissive look before waving his hand away. "I don't care. Go ahead and do it. We've been keeping it hidden for almost a year. "What's the use?"

Yanou was brought in by Mark. "I have to read you the statement I will be reading to the press, with your approval," she stated. She sat down at his bedside and began reading the manuscript in French-accented English. Her eyes welled up with tears as she talked. "Mr. Rock Hudson has developed acquired immune deficiency syndrome." The room was silent save for her voice, so quiet that every sound was amplified. A sheet was rustling. The hand on the wall clock began to tick. "Mr. Rock Hudson has acquired immune deficiency syndrome, which was diagnosed over a year ago in the United States."

The rock was immobile. He was watching the vision he had built die. He had planned, prepared, and protected his image as the romantic hero, the leading man, for thirty-six years. He had lived with the terror of being discovered for 36 years. Years of secretly exchanging phone numbers and sneaking out at three a.m. were passed. Years of chauffeuring attractive women to premieres before returning home to the man he lived with. Years of avoiding going out in public with "too many boys." Three years of marriage to a woman he thought he could love, but couldn't. Finally, following the societal revolutions of the 1960s and 1970s, and once Rock's stardom was assured, there was a period of rest. The press was aware of him and defended him. The entertainment industry was aware, but did not appear to care. Everyone would now be aware. Rock Hudson's identity would be revealed.

Perhaps the unburdening provided some relief. There would be no more stress or anxiety. He was able to let go. Life, career, and the globe were all over. What difference did it make? Rock had no idea, and couldn't even imagine, that with the death of the illusion, something new would be born.

Yanou had finished her reading. "Okay," Rock said after staring at her. "Go out there and feed it to the dogs."

Mark Miller stood outside a private conference room window, watching Yanou walk out to face the reporters on the hospital stairs. She read her statement aloud. They sat in startled silence. They hurried, knocking each other down, to the hospital phones once she finished. "He has AIDS," shouted a British woman. He's completed.``

Mark Miller was aware that the news was explosive, but he had not anticipated it being the lead item on the evening news around the world. Hundreds of telegrams and condolences were sent to Rock at the hospital within hours. Rock would get thirty thousand letters from admirers all throughout the world during the next two weeks. The content of the letters was much more startling than the numbers. People wrote, with rare exceptions, "Your private life is your own affair." We adore you and pray for you.

Mark was awoken that night by a phone call from Marc Christian in Los Angeles, who had seen the news on television and was outraged. Miller described the conversation as follows. "How dare you not tell me!" exclaimed Christian.

"It was up to Rock to tell you," Miller explained. It was Rock who had the sickness, not me. "Rock ordered that I not tell anyone."

"But why the hell didn't you tell me in the first place?" You should have informed me. I've been revealed. That's not fair!"

"I'm afraid I couldn't tell you," Mark admitted. "You are aware of my devotion to Rock Hudson. For the past 35 years, I have not been your friend. I attempted to provide hints. Remember how I asked you to get a full physical last year? The doctor who evaluated you was aware that you had been exposed to AIDS but found no evidence of it. "I doubt you have it right now." Miller assured him that they would take him to Paris right away so that Dr. Dormont could culture his blood.

When Mark arrived at Rock's room on Friday, July 26, he saw a glitter in his eye. "Are there any brush fires out there?"

"It's a firestorm," Mark declared.

"Thought it might be." With his finger, Rock formed a spiraling motion.

"I can't even leave my hotel room without being photographed," Mark explained. "I've turned into a minor media celebrity."

Rock burst out laughing. "Do you remember Andy Warhol saying that everyone should be famous for fifteen minutes?" You've been on sixteen now. [Get out]"

Rock's twinkle had returned, Mark reasoned, since Rock had always thrived in the midst of controversy. "He was happiest when putting out brush fires." Despite his protests that he despises attention, he understood the power of maintaining his name in print.

Mark informed him that Elizabeth Taylor had called and assured him that by coming forward and confessing he had AIDS, Rock would "save millions of lives."

"Why?" asked Rock.

Mark showed him telegrams from Frank Sinatra, Gregory Peck, Marlene Dietrich, James Garner, Carol Burnett, Ali MacGraw, Jack Lemmon, Richard Dreyfuss, Ava Gardner, Mickey Rooney, and Milton Berle, among others. One came from Madonna: "To Rock Hudson, my childhood sweetheart. I'm praying for you a lot. Madonna, I love you."

Rock was perplexed. "I'm not familiar with Madonna." Gregory Peck is someone I barely know."

Then there were the wires from motorcycle cops, switchboard employees, and instructors, all giving love and encouragement. Rock was perplexed because he had expected the opposite.

Rock's physicians concluded late Friday that he was strong enough to have a liver biopsy. The results would be available on Monday. Dr.

Dormont gave Rock two options: return to the United States, to UCLA Medical Center, and then return to Paris for treatment; or go to Percy Hospital and remain two to three weeks until he was in a situation where HPA 23 could be administered. "Think about it," remarked Dr. Dormont. "You can give me your answer on Sunday."

Yanou spent the weekend in St. Tropez, where she had a prior commitment to handle film publicity. Mark arrived at the hospital early Sunday morning and was greeted by the hospital's public relations director, Bruce Redor, as well as Dr. de Vernejoul and another specialist. They sat him down in the conference room and informed him that Rock was in critical condition. Whatever the biopsy revealed, Rock's white-cell count was so low that he would not survive. They predicted that he would die within three days. They requested that Mark inform Rock.

Mark agreed, but requested that they accompany him. Rock was sitting up in bed, anticipating Mark's arrival. Mark reached through the covers and grabbed his foot. "I'm afraid I have some bad news for you," he remarked. "You've only got three days to live."

"Oh, fuck." Rock moved his gaze to the window. He made the swirling motion with his finger that he used to suggest, ironically, "Whoopee." Then he looked at the men standing opposite him, who were grim-faced.

"What'll I do for an encore?"

They laughed because it relieved the strain and they were grateful.

"You can go to Percy Hospital," Mark recommended. "That has been resolved. "Or you could go to California..."

"I want to die in my own bed," stated Rock.

"You're on."

Mark asked whether he wanted to see his ex-wife, Phyllis Gates. Rock made a swaying motion with his palm, indicating that he wasn't sure.

"I'm leaving you with a mess," stated Rock. "And believe me, it's going to be a complete disaster." I apologize."

Mark paid little attention to that phrase or what it meant. He only had one mission: find a way to bring Rock home.

Mark called Yanou from St. Tropez on Sunday night, and they worked on chartering a plane all night and Monday. Because Rock required medical professionals and intensive-care equipment, a commercial trip was out of the question. They discovered a 707, but it couldn't fly to Los Angeles without making a stop. Europ Assistance proposed renting a 747 for $250,000, which included the intensive-care unit, doctors, and a nurse. Dr. Dormont stood up from his chair upon hearing the figure. "What? That is my research funding for the next four years!" Then he remembered: this was Rock's money, he earned it, and this was his final request.

Before the jet could take off, the funds had to be sent from New York. The wire was despatched, and the departure time was established for Monday at 11 p.m.

Yanou booked an ambulance to transport Rock from the hospital to the nearby heliport. To deflect public attention, she issued a statement stating that Rock was stable and would remain in the hospital for another week. It rained Monday evening, and there were no reporters present when the ambulance arrived with Rock. Dr. Dormont and Dr. de Vernejoul followed in their own vehicle. They said their goodbyes to Yanou as Rock was taken to the helicopter. "I don't think we can be of any further assistance."

Rock was dozing out after being given a sedative. The chopper landed beyond customs at Charles de Gaulle Airport, where photographs were not permitted. Rock was taken onto the 747 on a stretcher, which was laid across a row of seats.

When Rock awoke, he noticed Yanou standing next to him.

"Where am I?"

"Rock, you're on your way back to Los Angeles," she added.

"Am I really flying?"

"No, not yet." You'll be flying in forty minutes."

"Who's on board with me?" He took a look around. "Where's Mark?"

"Mark is not present. He needs to stay in Paris to pay bills and handle paperwork. He'll be back the following day."

Rock appeared disoriented.

"Be happy," remarked Yanou. "On the other side, everyone is waiting for you. Dale Olson is present... your doctor..."

"But, how did I get on a plane?"

"Listen, I'll explain." Yanou explained how she rented the ambulance, rented the helicopter, lied to the press, and landed with the aircraft past customs. "So we can avoid all of the press!"

Rock began to chuckle--the deep, rippling laugh that had so captivated his buddies. "I love that," he exclaimed. "Fuck the press."

When the nurse passed by, Rock questioned Yanou, "Who is she?"

"That's the nurse accompanying you."

"She's very pretty."

"Rock, please don't start, because I am very jealous," Yanou begged.

"But...you're flying with me, aren't you?"

"No, I cannot."

"You're not coming with me, either?"

She apologized and said that she had business responsibilities.

Rock began to cry.

He was alone on a deserted jumbo plane, surrounded by two physicians and a nurse who didn't understand his language. Yanou grasped his hand, but he stopped crying after a moment.

He swallowed and regained command. He laughed. "You know, it would have been fantastic if you could have joined me on the flight. The chocolate mousse could have been created at my house."

She gave him a peck on the cheek.

Rock glanced at her in awe. "You're really not afraid... to touch me?" He motioned to her hand in his.

"No," she replied.

The flight attendant approached. "The plane is prepared. We're free to go."

Rock told Yanou, "I'll call you when I get home."

The jet touched down in Los Angeles about one a.m. on Tuesday, July 30. There were no intimate friends present to meet Rock, only the reporters, who were kept at a safe distance. He was flown by helicopter to UCLA, where he resided for a month before returning to the Castle, where he would die in his own bed, just as he had requested.

Chapter 2

Many years later, Rock Hudson informed friends that he had been aware of his attraction to guys since he was nine years old. There had been a pleasant event with an older man on a farm where he was visiting. Roy, in fact, had supported it. "But I was convinced that I was the only guy who felt the way I did." He became increasingly aware of his sexuality while serving in the military, when he had multiple interactions with males, but they were always secretive and dangerous.

When Rock sailed out of the Golden Gate to begin his tour, Doris Day's voice came over the ship's loudspeakers singing "Sentimental Journey." The seamen had stopped talking. They were eighteen-year-olds set to go on a voyage to war, and Doris was singing about the journey home. "She had the whole ship in tears, including me," Roy remarked.

He couldn't have imagined that thirteen years later, he'd be on screen with Doris Day in one of the era's most successful comedies. That he and Doris would be a team--the personification of everything beautiful and true about a man and a woman. The voice on the speakers, Doris Day, was as far away from Seaman Roy Fitzgerald as the moon.

Rock Hudson told me before he died the following anecdote about how he obtained his moniker from his first agent, Henry Willson:

Henry was convinced he understood what was best for me. I recall his saying, "We have to change your name."

"Why?" I inquired. "I don't want one of those silly names."

"You have to, so it looks good on the marquee," he remarked. "Roy Fitzgerald is overly long."

"What about Geraldine Fitzgerald?" says one. Is that too much time?"

But Henry was adamant. He smacked me with Hudson. He also had some macho, cockamamie first names. Dirk, for example. Lance. He finally said, "What about Rock?" That made sense. "Yeah, that sounds pretty good," I admitted. It was close to Roy, and no one else had it. That was the end of it.

Rock recounted this story so many times and in so many different ways that it became part of the Rock Hudson canon. However, long after Hudson's death, I got a letter from Herbert Millspaugh, a retired clerk in San Francisco, who claimed to have been present the day Roy Fitzgerald was given the name Rock Hudson. He gave names, dates, and images to back up his claims.

Millspaugh claimed that in the summer of 1947, he was living in Long Beach, working for the Texas Oil Company, hanging out at the Villa Riviera, and attending parties at Ken Hodge's penthouse. Ken introduced him to Roy Fitzgerald, a really attractive young man he'd recently met who wanted to be an actor. One Sunday, a bunch of Ken's buddies returned from the beach to Ken's apartment, poured gin and tonics, and began brainstorming names for the actor. When most stars first started out, they changed their names as part of the process of being reborn, of bringing a romantic character to life.

"Ken wanted a name that suggested strength," Millspaugh explained. "Someone suggested Rock. Then we searched through the Long Beach phone directory for another name that sounded familiar. Hudson was the name we came up with. Everything you've read in the press over the previous four decades concerning the name's origin is nonsense. It all started on that long Sunday afternoon in Long Beach."

According to Millspaugh, Roy Fitzgerald and Ken Hodge went from Long Beach to Hollywood and shared a bungalow in the hills. Ken began making use of his relationships, throwing parties to introduce Roy to individuals in the business. At one occasion, Henry Willson appeared, grabbed Roy aside, and instructed him to call him at his office--he was David 0. Selznick Studio's chief of talent. "And when he left," Millspaugh added, "he had signed a contract, which Ken had not thought to do with his protege." Ken returned to Long Beach and went to pieces once Henry Willson became Roy's agent.``

Rock Hudson told many accounts about meeting Henry Willson. He told one reporter that he used to be a mail carrier and noticed Henry Willson on his route, so he gave him a picture of himself. He said he sent his images to hundreds of agents, directors, and producers, and only one of them called him-Willson. Rock was signed after attending an interview.

Because Ken Hodge, Henry Willson, and Rock Hudson are no longer alive, there is no one to confirm the story. But when Millspaugh's letter arrived, I read it aloud to Mark Miller and George Nader. They exchanged looks. "It sounds like Rock," Mark commented. He went to the folders and pulled out the first acting check Rock had received. He had never cashed it for sentimental reasons. Vanguard Films, Inc., Culver City, issued a ten-dollar check to Roy Fitzgerald on March 19, 1948. The check was written soon after Rock joined with Willson.

ROY FITZGERALD PAY TO THE ORDER OF ROCK HUDSON was written on the back. HODGE, KENNETH G.

The Selznick Studio was disbanding when Henry met Rock, and Henry intended to form his own talent agency. He signed with Rock, who warned him up front that he had no training. Henry enrolled him in evening acting classes and started scheduling interviews and screen tests for him.

The big studios held screen tests to determine whether or not to sign a fresh actor to a contract. Rock was tested five times with no offers. He was immature and overeager, like the amateur who smiles even though a gun is aimed at him. Twentieth Century-Fox still shows one of the screen tests to young actors as an example of how horrible one can be and still become a star through hard work.

Undaunted, Henry took Rock to meet Raoul Walsh, a Warner Brothers director. Raoul wore a patch over one eye, and friends theorized that Raoul saw Rock through the same lens as the camera. Raoul cast Rock in Fighter Squadron as a bit part and informed him the picture would serve as a screen test because of his appearance. Jimmy Matteoni, a rock in Winnetka, was giddy with delight. "I've got a role!" I'm going to make a hundred and twenty dollars per week. I'm wealthy. Rich!" He called Budget Pack and walked out.

Rock had three lines in Fighter Squadron as an air corps officer. In the squadron's recreation room, he had to explain, "Pretty soon you're going to have to get a bigger blackboard." The harder he tried, the more tongue twisted he became, until after twenty takes, they modified the phrase to "Pretty soon you'll have to write smaller numbers." But Rock looked stunning on the big screen. "He had a face that the camera liked," a buddy remarked. "He appeared ten times better on screen or in a still photo than in person." It was his expression. You can learn to come alive on television, but the camera needs to say, 'This is a truly gorgeous or handsome person,' and it has to be in the face.``

Raoul Walsh signed Rock to a one-year contract following Fighter Squadron, which would cover his living expenses while he studied acting.

During that year, I began attending classes and diction lessons, learning how to lower my voice... learning whatever I could. Because something in my midwestern hick idiocy told me that if you're going to do something, do it. And do your absolute best.

Young actors now frequently ask me, "How do you approach a scene?" You just do it/ Raoul Walsh's attitude was "you just do it." When he stated that, it made everything so clear in my mind.

He advised not to try to act. Remember, you're magnified forty times on that screen. It will look fantastic if you are natural and understated.

Sophie Rosenstein, a talented teacher who held the capacity to draw out each person's natural skills, conducted Rock acting workshops. Sophie would screen old Garbo movies without sound on Saturday mornings. She claimed that if you viewed movies without sound, you could tell whether someone was acting or faking it.

Rock learned to fence, work weights in the gym, and ride horses on the back lot. "I've even studied ballet," he revealed. Lester Luther, a vocal coach, taught him a technique for reducing his speaking voice. He urged Rock to stand at the piano and yell as loudly as he could, ideally when he had a cold or throat illness. This was believed to weaken the vocal chords, resulting in a lower voice when they healed. The procedure damaged Rock's singing voice, but it gave him the unusually deep, sensuous voice that became his signature.

The wardrobe crew created a dummy of him and dressed him in a tuxedo and suits. There would be no more too-short pants. The new clothing was part of the Studio's total makeover. Roy Fitzgerald stepped in off the street, went through makeup, clothes, hair, tutoring, and PR, and emerged as rising new actor Rock Hudson. He learned how to go into a restaurant like a celebrity, how to exit a limousine like a celebrity, how to grin while keeping his eyes open, and how to walk down a staircase without looking down. "If you're hungry, don't walk to the commissary," Rock was instructed, "you call a car."

Rock was cast in minor roles while he studied. He'd gone from driving a truck to acting on a soundstage, learning as he went. He listened to everyone--script girls advised him on how to read lines, and electricians advised him on where to stand for optimum lighting. His agreement was for seven years. The Studio chose which films he would appear in and paid him $75 per week whether he appeared in one or a dozen. He worked forty weeks and took a twelve-week break, but he couldn't find a job elsewhere. If he decided to do a film for a different studio, Universal would give him three months off, but they would add six months to the end of his contract. He was given raises on a regular basis, and the Studio had the option of terminating him after a year.

Some actors considered these contracts to be "slavery," while Rock thought it was a fantastic arrangement. "Everything was handled by the Studio. They could get you a house, a car, plane tickets, and designer shoes. All you needed to do was focus on your performance. There was no better way to train.

The goal of all the training and grooming was to create stars-properties-that would generate revenue for the Studio. Publicity was critical, and Universal kept a big crew of publicists on hand to keep the players' names in the news. Rock was expected to attend premieres and nightclubs with young actresses under contract in order for both of their images to appear in the article. Another promotional strategy was the design of a fan magazine. Rock would be requested to stage a "date" with an actress and bring along a photographer to picture them as they played tennis on the beach or danced at Ciro's, peering into each other's eyes.

Vera Ellen, a dancer under contract to M.G.M., was one of the actresses Rock was paired with in the publications. Vera Ellen was more well-known and older than Rock, so she was able to persuade him to come up with her. They came up with the notion of dressing up in tight bathing costumes, painting their bodies gold, and attending the Hollywood Press Photographers Ball as Mr. and Mrs. Oscar in 1950. It was audacious, and every photographer raced and jostled to get their shot. Vera was brought to the microphone by Louella Parsons, who was doing a live radio show from the event. She brought Rock along, which is how he received his first national radio interview with Louella.

Going out with Vera had been a cunning professional maneuver, but Rock grew to care for her and even considered marriage at one point. He reminded Jimmy Matteoni that they had agreed to be best men at each other's weddings. But as Rock and Vera grew apart, her career began to wane while Rock's continued to soar.

When Rock arrived at Universal, it was a tight-knit studio where the same people worked on picture after picture. Rock enjoyed going out to eat with his makeup artist, wardrobe man, and a script lady, Betty Abbott, who was Bud Abbott's niece. "You knew everyone by first name," Rock remarked, "from the carpenters to the Studio head." You never shut your door. It was a group."

Chapter 3

Magnificent Obsession was my first solid dramatic part in which I didn't have to rely on my body. Now I give credit to the Studio... They put me in all of those western and Indian movies to train me. Whereas if my dramatic scenes weren't all that great, it didn't really matter. I was aware of this, so I experimented with various methods to see if they would work. And I'd say, "Oh, no, no. "Don't do that again" or "Take that a step further." And it was a fantastic experience. So when Magnificent Obsession rolled along, I was prepared.

While getting to know Mark Miller and George Nader, Rock was not romantically involved with anyone and did not want to be. With that in mind, Mark and George, who had moved to a beachfront property in Venice, invited Rock to dinner with a young guy they'd met, Jack Navaar, in 1952. Jack was floating after returning from his service in Korea. He met Henry Willson, who volunteered to represent him and attempted to change his name to Rand Saxon.

Jack was twenty-two years old. He'd been hearing "You should be in pictures" his entire life. He was tall, slim, and fit, with blond wavy hair, blue eyes, and a heart-shaped face that was finely carved. He also had a bright mind and a caustic wit. "When I heard Rock Hudson, the Rock Hudson, was coming," he remembers, "I was nervous, kind of excited, and a little embarrassed." Rock arrived, but sat in a corner and said nothing. Jack entered the kitchen, where Mark was preparing dinner. "I don't think he likes me," Jack said. "He isn't even speaking to me. "I think I should go home." He had canceled a date with a woman to attend supper. Mark advised him to give it a shot.

Rock was silent at dinner, but he startled everyone when he said, "Let's go up to my place and listen to records." They went up to Rock's place on Avenida del Sol since he had just purchased an exciting hi-fi system. "It was thrilling for me because it was way up in the hills and had a view like nothing I'd ever seen," Jack explains. Mark began turning down lights, establishing the ambiance, and "playing matchmaker" while Bob Preble was out, and then he and George snuck away.

Rock and Jack stayed up late talking, joking, and listening to music. "Is it easy for you, do you usually get what you want in life?" Rock inquired.

"I don't know," Jack said. "I'm not sure what I want exactly."

"That is the most difficult thing for me." to obtain something when I truly desire it."

"What exactly do you mean?"

"Well, I'd like to invite you to stay with me tonight. I'd like to get to know you better, but I'm really sabotaging it...

"No, you are not," Jack stated emphatically.

The following morning, Rock prepared breakfast. He liked to cook "Greyhound Bus Station Eggs"--cracking eggs directly into the skillet and scrambling them quickly so the white and yellow didn't mix--along with loads of toast, bacon, fresh orange juice, and coffee. He and Jack spent the day together, and Rock called Mark and George in the evening. "Hiya! "What are you up to tonight?" He shocked them by taking Jack back down to the beach for another dinner. Rock saw Jack four or five evenings a week from then on.

Rock's pursuit of Jack was flattering and exciting, but he was not fully comfortable in a homosexual relationship. When I met Jack in 1985, he was married to a younger lady, they had three small children, and they were thinking about having a fourth. Jack had started his own clothes company. They resided in a nice home in a remote area of Southern California, complete with a white fence and five pumpkins on the porch for Halloween. They rode horses and kept four behind the house in a corral.

"And in those days, if you had sex with a man, that put you in a category from which you couldn't deviate," Jack recalled of his high school homosexual connection. You were supposed to be a fruitcake your entire life. But I'd had relationships with women before, and a part of me still wanted to."

His parents were divorcing when he met Rock; "my family was falling apart, and Rock made me feel secure and loved." When Preble moved out of Avenida del Sol in May 1953, Rock and Jack began living together. They did, however, find a new home, a two-story house on Grandview, because, as Jack explained to Rock, "I don't want to live in the same house where you lived with Bob."

Rock urged Jack to quit his job at Hughes Aircraft so he could be home and free when Rock was free. After a week of shooting, Rock would remark, "Let's drive to the Grand Canyon." They'd pack a few belongings in the car and drive away, staying in motels or camping out before daring each other to swim in a freezing creek. "We lived a reclusive life and were very involved with each other," Jack explains. They went to the movies all the time, and Rock's favorite actress was Lana Turner. They played a game called "Last Word." Julia Adams would call, say "last word," and then hang up, never answering the phone. As a result, Rock and Jack sent her a telegram with the words "last word." They also played "Gotcha," in which they attempted to scare one other. "One person would hide in the closet, the other would come in to reach for a shirt, and you'd jump out and yell 'Gotcha!'" explains Jack. You'd be surprised at how many times you'd fall for it and shout. You'd let your guard down, stroll outside to empty the garbage, and get caught. Perhaps this is why both of us had heart attacks later in life."

They had a secret code that read "1-2-3," which meant "I love you." When there were other people around, Rock would rap three times on a counter, bump Jack three times under the table, or yell "One two three." "He was a very romantic man," says Jack, "and I responded to it."

They would dress up on Sundays and alternate between going to see Rock's mother, who lived in Arcadia with her third husband, Joe Olson, and Jack's mother, who resided in Santa Monica. Rock's mother referred to Jack as "Cookie," and she made roast lamb with mint jelly because she felt Jack would enjoy it. Finally, Jack asked Kay if she could manufacture another item. "Of course, Cookie," Kay assured her. "I despise lamb." "I was preparing it for you."

Rock organized a celebration for Jack's twenty-third birthday and gave him a heap of presents--boxes piled upon boxes--from an upscale Beverly Hills boutique, Gifts for Men. "There was a yellow and a black cashmere sweater, as well as belts, socks, and shirts." He was like a child, and he enjoyed giving gifts."

Rock was supporting Jack after he left Hughes Aircraft, which Jack liked and disliked. "I had credit cards and there was always cash on the table for me to take." Rock paid for my mother's divorce; I needed money to maintain my mother and two sisters, so Rock gave me some. But I despised him for it because it made me feel like I had no balls. I couldn't bear being reliant. I was angry if he did lovely things for me, and even worse if he didn't do pleasant things and ignored me. "I was a rage-filled young man."

Jack attended acting lessons during the hours Rock worked, which Rock paid for. "Henry Willson would set up interviews, but I always got the impression he was doing it for Rock." "What are the movie stars' wives doing today?" Mark Miller would ask. "Should we have lunch at the Beverly Hills Hotel?" While Rock and George were on site, Jack and Mark began to hang around. The four would then meet together in the evening.

One night, Rock and Mark announced that they had a surprise for them. They went into the bedroom, asking George to switch up the record player, and when the music started, out came Rock and Mark, dressed only in two neckties tied around their waists like bikini tops and bottoms. Rosemary Clooney and Marlene Dietrich were performing a duet, and Rock and Mark performed a dance while mouthing the words, "I want your name, age, height, and size... Mark played Rosemary Clooney, while Rock played Marlene. George began to giggle, but Jack cried, "Stop! Switch it off. It's not amusing!"

"I didn't like anything to do with drag or camp," Jack recalls of the experience. "I didn't like gay humor." He was mortified, he adds, if Rock wanted to hold his hand while driving or if they were at the movies and Rock called him "Baby." "I was afraid that the people behind us might hear," Jack explains.

Rock was tested for the lead in his first major film, Magnificent Obsession, shortly after he and Jack began living together. Douglas Sirk, the filmmaker, had already signed Jane Wyman, who was then married to Ronald Reagan. Sirk felt compelled to create one because Universal didn't have many prominent male actors under contract. He witnessed Iron Man and subsequently commented, "He was far inferior to Jeff Chandler, but I thought I saw something." So I set up a meeting with him, and he appeared to be not too much to the eye, except incredibly attractive. However, the camera sees with its own eyes. It detects things that the human eye does not. You learn to trust your camera because it's the only thing in Hollywood that has never failed me."

He wanted Rock to do eight scenes--two days of extensive testing-- and then he and the producer, Ross Hunter, went over the picture. They decided Rock was ready for the lead part. Magnificent

Obsession was a remake of a 1935 film starring Robert Taylor and Irene Dunne, which was based on Lloyd C. Douglas' romance novel of the same name. Rock portrayed Bob Merrick, a greedy, swaggering playboy at the start of the story. When the technician cautions him that the lake conditions are unsafe, he sneers, "You keep this engine tuned, that's all I want from you." Merrick nearly drowns after cracking up the boat. He is rescued by an emergency crew, but while he is being treated, Dr. Wayne Phillips dies on the opposite side of the lake due to a lack of emergency equipment.

Dr. Phillips was the polar antithesis of Merrick: humble and selfless in his dedication to humanity. Merrick meets his widow, Jane Wyman, and falls in love with her. He also meets an eccentric painter who was a doctor's acquaintance and tells Merrick, "He connected me to the infinite source of power." The procedure for obtaining this power is simple: find someone in need of assistance, assist him, keep it a secret, and never ask to be paid back.

Hudson attempts the approach and also chases Wyman, but she rushes away and is hit by a car, leaving her blind. Hudson pays her medical fees in secret and arranges for her to travel to Europe for surgery, which fails. He spends time with her while posing as someone else. They fall in love, but when she discovers who he is, she disappears.

Hudson attends medical school and eventually becomes Dr. Phillips, performing unselfish service. After several years, he is summoned to operate on Wyman in order to save her life. He is terrified, but the painter is there to comfort him with a 1950s rendition of "May the force be with you." Wyman lives and sees after the operation.

What's astonishing about the film is how Rock is transformed from sinner to saint, from rogue to gentle knight, practically instantly. He becomes entirely wholesome, completely loving, and his expression of that love is plain and uncomplicated. There are no doubting shadows to guide you to their twisted and dark depths. He may have been gruff and unpleasant at first, but in the end, he is a nice, good-hearted all-American man.

When Douglas Sirk first read the script, he thought, "This is a damned crazy story if ever there was one." The woman's blindness. The irony of it all... it's a mix of kitsch, crazy, and trashiness. But crazy is crucial, since it protects trashy crap like Magnificent Obsession. This is the dialectic: there is a very short distance between high art and rubbish, and trash with an element of madness is, by definition, closer to art."

In August 1953, two weeks before filming began, Rock and Jack spent the day with Mark and George in Laguna. They packed huge black inner tubes to ride the waves, but the surf was severe, and Rock was tossed onto the rocks by a wave. He fainted when his collar bone was fractured. George carried him up the steps to the promenade, while Mark dashed to the Coast Inn's bar. "We've had an accident, and I'm in desperate need of brandy!" He brought the brandy back, and to everyone's surprise, Jack drank it down. They phoned an ambulance and then the Studio. Rock was distraught and begged Jack to accompany him in the ambulance. "I don't think I should, I'll ride in the car with Mark and George," Jack protested, but Rock urged. They were transported to the Studio first, where a doctor examined Rock before transporting him to St. Joseph's Hospital. Rock was devastated when the crack was discovered. "How long will it take for me to heal?" I have to start working on a picture in two weeks." He was frightened of losing the part if they had to postpone production due to him. The part was a game changer; he might not have another chance.

The doctors gave him two options: insert a pin into the bone and cast his arm and shoulder for six weeks, or set the bone and wrap an Ace bandage around his arm and chest to hold his shoulders back. He could return to work in two weeks with the latter, but he would have a huge lump--a calcium deposit--on his shoulder that would not heal completely. Rock chose the Ace bandage without hesitation.

After the accident, a faction at Universal attempted to have him removed from the film, but Rock had an ally who stopped them. Rock had begun an illicit affair with one of the Studio's most senior executives, a short, paunchy man who was married and had three children. Rock told his pals about how the executive would lock his office door, have his secretary take the calls, and then come running after him on his knees. Rock didn't see him very often, but it was enough to keep the executive interested and willing to assist Rock's cause. With this alliance, Rock was able to persuade the studio to loan him to Warner Brothers for Giant and Twentieth Century-Fox for A Farewell to Arms. Thirty years later, after retiring and having dozens of grandchildren, the CEO ran across Rock at a cocktail party. He sought a quiet opportunity to pull Rock aside and say, softly, "I still love you."

Rock began Magnificent Obsession on time, despite having a damaged shoulder. It was shot in Lake Arrowhead, and Rock would drive home on weekends to see Jack. They collaborated on scenes and got drunk to prepare for a drunken scene in the film. "We read the lines to each other and asked each other questions about how we felt and perceived things," Jack explains. "We discovered that a drunk does not act drunk; rather, he attempts to appear sober."

Rock wanted to do his best and received assistance from Sirk and Wyman.

Douglas Sirk put me under his wing, and I'm grateful. He was like a father to me, and I was like a son to him, I believe. When you're afraid and new and trying to figure out what you're doing, an older man will suddenly reach out and say, "There, there, it's okay." Sirk was Douglas Sirk.

Jane Wyman couldn't have been more pleasant... Jane was aware of my inexperience, anxiety, and nervousness. And I'd go high; I'd go over my lines thirty or forty times. She'd never say anything. "Fine, fine, fine."

Many years later, she stated something fascinating to me. "You went out of your way, Jane, to be nice to me when you didn't have to," I replied. I want you to know that I am aware of this and appreciate it. And I admire you for it. "Thank you very much." "Let me tell you something," she said. It was given to me by someone. I also gave it to you. "Now it's your turn to pass it on to someone else."

The Studio staged a sneak showing of Magnificent Obsession at the Valley's Four Star Theatre to gauge crowd reaction. When Rock and Jack learned about it, they crept inside the theater and sat in the back row, surrounded by unknowing moviegoers. When the movie ended, Rock bolted from the theater. Jack got lost in the crowd, and when he found Rock, he was filled with emotion in his car in the parking lot. Rock was crying, his head pressed against the steering wheel. He realized he was a celebrity at that time. He had achieved the pinnacle, the lofty state he had imagined, the place that had appeared completely out of reach for a boy from the Midwest with no training and no contacts. Yet there he was, on the big screen, with an Academy Award-winning actress and a chorus and orchestra performing Beethoven's Ninth Symphony's "Ode to Joy."

"You were really great," Jack replied.

"Thank you, thank you," he cried out.

"You know it too, don't you?" Jack spoke softly.

Rock laughed while still crying.

"I'm very proud of you."

On May 11, 1954, Klieg lights illuminated the sky as Rock Hudson arrived at the Westwood Theater for the premiere of Magnificent Obsession. Betty Abbott was his date; Jack Navaar arrived in a separate car, dressed in George Nader's tuxedo and escorting a young actress, Claudia Boyer.

"Rock! Rock! Rock!" Please turn around! Please take a moment to look this way!" As the strobe lights flashed, bright sparks illuminated Rock's eyes.

"Can you tell me the name of your date, Rock?" "Are you married?"

Rock noticed Jack Navaar's mother and two little sisters standing behind the rope barriers with the fans as he walked up the red carpet. He defied his rank to approach them and kiss them. Years later, Jack recalled, "Rock didn't have to do it-that's why I couldn't help but love him."

Rock had told Jack that he wanted him to sit next to him in the theater, but they were assigned to opposite sections. Rock and Betty sat with Ross Hunter and Jane Wyman, while Jack and Claudia had to sit with Jacque Mapes and Ann Sheridan in a less favorable location. Jack was enraged and refused to speak to Rock for the remainder of the evening. He hesitated to look Rock in the eyes at the post-film celebration at La Rue's. They brought their dates home and met at the house.

"You said we'd be sitting together," Jack pointed out. "I felt like a dummy. It's as though you're the star and I'm the jerk!"

Ross Hunter, according to Rock, had adjusted the seats at the last minute. He was startled when Magnificent Obsession grossed $8 million, making Rock Hudson Universal's most profitable performer. Every week, he received three thousand pieces of fan mail. A woman in Tacoma, Washington, wrote, "When you looked at Jane Wyman, I wanted to scream, and deep down inside of me, I did." Rock rose from B movies to the top of the double bill, and was stereotyped as the romantic leading man. He would not be cast in Tennessee Williams' works, and he would not play damaged souls. He was square-Mr. Right, heroic, and attractive.

Everyone treated Rock differently after Magnificent Obsession. "A lot of people say I've changed, but I haven't," he informed Mark and George. Others have shifted to me. I used to be thought of as a movie star, but now people gaze at me with their mouths open in... complete wonder." But Rock did evolve. "Before, Rock would answer the phone, 'Hiya!'" adds Mark. It was now deep, 'Hello? Rock Hudson is speaking.' He instantly became an authority on everything. He was able to walk on water."

Jack Navaar saw as Rock abandoned his shyness and began to revel in the spotlight. "If Rock burped, everyone laughed hysterically, as if it was the greatest burp they'd ever heard." In an interview with Hedda Hopper, Rock discussed the transformation from insecurity to confidence. "Being tall--I was six feet by the time I was fourteen-- gives you a sense of inferiority. I believe I began to come out of it when people recognized me. 'You are, after all, Rock Hudson, aren't you?' What the Hell! I thought to myself. I had nothing to hide, so I stood up."

National magazines were suddenly writing about rock. Rock was shown dangling from the top of a ladder with Tony Curtis and Robert Wagner below him in a Life feature on the hottest male actors in 1954. Rock was said to rank third in the box office with females under the age of twenty. According to Life, his appeal "lies primarily in his basic honesty or in his bare chest."

The fan publications began to worry about Hudson's lack of marriage. They had to continue presenting him to their audience as "eligible husband material." How can one explain the fact that he was never romantically involved with any of the attractive women he brought to parties? How many times could they show him with Betty Abbott or Marilyn Maxwell and say, "Friends say they may be getting serious"? They addressed the issue by printing headlines such as SCARED OF MARRIAGE? and TOO TIRED FOR LOVE. "I'm looking for happiness," said Rock, "but I don't think I'm quite ready for marriage yet." The inference was that he hadn't met the right girl yet.

Confidential, another magazine, was interested in Rock's single status. Unlike the fan magazines, Confidential published scandalous articles about celebrities, many of which were fictitious. TELLS THE FACTS AND NAMES THE NAMES was its logo. WHY ROBERT WAGNER IS A FLAT TIRE IN A BOUDOIR and

WHEN LANA TURNER SHARED A LOVER WITH AVA GARDNER were headlines that promised more than the stories delivered.

Confidential intended to expose Rock's homosexuality and offered Bob Preble money in exchange for information and photographs. Someone from the magazine eventually offered Jack Navaar $10,000 (a considerable sum in 1954) to talk about living with Rock. Jack called Henry Willson and informed him that Confidential was looking for Rock. "We're aware of that," Willson stated. "Many thanks for your help."

No story was ever published, and the rumor inside Universal was that the studio had exchanged material about another of its stars, Rory Calhoun, in order to kill the piece on Rock. In the mid-1950s, it was reported that Calhoun had served time in prison for burglary and auto theft when he was younger. However, whether there was a link between the Calhoun tales and the impending Rock expose cannot be proven.

There was recently a report that the Studio surrendered a story about George Nader's sexuality to Confidential in order to save Rock's career. But this is not the case. No item concerning George Nader's sexuality appeared in Confidential or any other journal, and he continued to perform until his retirement in 1972.

"We lived in fear of an expose, or even one small remark, a veiled suggestion that someone was homosexual," adds Nader. Such a comment would have shook the Studio to its core. Every month, when Confidential was released, our stomachs turned. Which of us would participate? The amazing thing is that, despite his fame, Rock was never nailed. Because he appeared to be under supernatural protection, I speculated that Rock had an angel on his shoulder or had made a contract with the devil."

During this time, Rock and Jack began to argue more regularly. "I couldn't go anywhere with Rock--even to dinner--without people staring and trying to approach him," Jack adds. "I was envious of his acclaim and attention, but I also liked it." Thousands of others desired him, but Rock Hudson preferred me."

Jack claims he frequently created confrontations and gave Rock "every reason to throw me out." I literally booted him out of bed one night." Rock had been encouraged by Jack to socialize more because it was helpful for his profession. Rock accepted a date to accompany

Joan Crawford to a party, but returned home around three a.m. "I'd been worried about him, and he came home stinking drunk," Jack explains. "I was upset because he was with Joan Crawford and I wasn't." When we got into bed, he began snoring, and I became so enraged that I rolled over and kicked him to the floor. I told him to get out of the house since I didn't care where he slept." Rock began going down Grandview Drive, and Jack threw the car keys after him. "I told him to go to sleep in his big fucking plush dressing room that the Studio had just built for him."

When the dust settled, Rock asked Jack, "Would you be happy if I gave up all this shit?" "We'll relocate to the Midwest." No, Jack said. "Rock wasn't serious, and I didn't want to move to Chicago with Roy Fitzgerald and open a florist shop." I wanted Rock to have a career, but I also wanted one."

Rock told Mark Miller about an incident with Jack that got him so upset that he used it in other films when he needed to summon wrath. Rock had stayed late at the Studio. When he called home, Jack stated he didn't think Rock was working. Rock's record collection would be thrown over the hillside if he didn't return home in thirty minutes. Rock got home from work, saw Jack flinging his 78 records of Ella Fitzgerald, Nat King Cole, Dinah Shore, and Duke Ellington over the deck, and heard them shatter on the rocks below. Rock went insane. He told Mark, "All I have to do to get insanely angry is visualize those records flying down the hill." Jack Navaar claims he has no recollection of the incident.

Rock left for Europe in June 1954 to film Captain Lightfoot. Jack drove Rock to the airport and escorted him to his flight. When Rock took his position by the window, he flashed their code: 1-2-3, using the overhead light. I adore you.

Rock traveled to Paris and met Betty Abbott, the screenplay girl for the picture, and his co-star, Barbara Rush. They only had two weeks until shooting started, so they rented a big American automobile with plenty of legroom for Rock, and he drove the three of them around France and Italy. They stayed in modest hotels and would stop in the countryside at lunch to lay a blanket and have a picnic with wine, cheese, and fruit. Rock was studying wine and European cuisine, as well as art and opera, architecture, and history. He was constantly reading and absorbing all he saw. He loved Florence, especially the Uffizi Gallery and Michelangelo's David statue.

While Rock was traveling through Europe, Jack Navaar met Phyllis Gates, a young woman who worked as a secretary for Henry Willson. Jack had met Phyllis in Henry's office and the two of them had begun going out to lunch. "I had a tremendous crush on Phyllis," Jack admits. "I could see why Rock thought he could fall in love with her; I could have." She knows how to make a man feel fantastic. 'No, honey, you don't want to eat that for lunch; you should have this because it's better for you,' she'd remark. She was far more lovely in person than in her images, and she had a wonderful laugh and a fantastic personality--you'd meet her and feel like you were the most important person in her life in 10 minutes. It was a gift."

On Sundays, they would go to the Tropical Village in Santa Monica, which was popular with gay men and lesbians. Jack and Mark took Phyllis to Laguna one weekend while Rock and George Nader were on site. When they went to Camille's on the first night, Phyllis began talking to a woman, and Jack and Mark did not see her again for the remainder of the weekend. "We'd call her room and invite her to dinner or the beach, and she'd say, 'You go ahead, I'll catch up,'" Mark remembers.

Phyllis had two weeks off over the summer, so Henry Willson called Jack and suggested, "Why don't you and Phyllis go on a trip?" The rock is gone, and you're just sitting there. Phyllis wishes to pay a visit to her relatives." Jack consented, and they drove across the Rockies in Rock's new yellow Lincoln Continental convertible to Montevideo, Minnesota, where Phyllis's family lived. "I liked her company, and I felt safe doing it because Henry suggested it," Jack adds. "Later, I realized Henry had instigated the trip in order to alienate me from Rock."

To save money, they stayed in motels as Mr. and Mrs. Navaar, sharing a room but not sleeping together, according to Jack. They sang popular songs while driving, their favorite being "Little Things Mean a Lot." As they approached Montevideo, Phyllis stated, "They had to swear--they had to yell every dirty word they knew and get it out of their systems because they wouldn't be able to do it at all in Montevideo.""So we cursed, shouted, and cussed for ten minutes," Jack recounts.

They remained with her family, and all of her family and friends came to meet "Rock Hudson's roommate" and to see "Rock Hudson's car." They then proceeded to Kansas City, where Phyllis had worked as a flight attendant before moving to California. Phyllis took Jack to homosexual parties where ladies kissed and danced together. When they arrived in Los Angeles, Jack discovered he was in serious difficulty. Rock called, angry and accusatory, from Venice, Italy. He'd heard that Jack was throwing drinking parties in the house; that Jack had left the house unprotected and it had been looted; that police had been called repeatedly; and that Jack had been observed driving Rock's Lincoln convertible full of rowdy people chanting obscenities.

"I wasn't even in town!" he exclaimed. Jack stated. "You son of a bitch, how dare you ask me those questions."

The more Rock questioned him, the angrier Jack became, and the long-distance call ended in disaster. When Jack called Rock's business manager, he was told that no more money was available for him. Jack appealed to Henry Willson, but Henry hinted that Rock and Jack's connection was jeopardizing Rock's job and that it would be better if it terminated. "The Studio is capable of taking extreme measures to protect a property," stated Willson.

"Everyone, including Phyllis, turned on me." "She vanished," Jack replies. "Everyone treated me like I was a piece of dead meat. I felt like dead meat, and I didn't want to be that way for the rest of my life. So I did exactly what they asked of me. I left the keys at Henry's office and left."

When Rock returned from Europe, he discovered that the house on Grandview had been stripped of any signs of Jack Navaar. Rock had begun living with Jack before he became famous. Rock became more careful after Jack left. "He went deep into the closet and didn't come out for fourteen years," Mark Miller explains. Rock would not live with a guy again until the late 1960s, when social prejudices had softened and his celebrity appeared secure.

Chapter 4

Rock felt he had to own the mansion on Beverly Crest Drive, but he lacked the funds to do it. When his contract expired in 1962, Universal used it as a bargaining chip: if he renewed, they would give him the house. Don Morgan, a publicist and friend of Rock's, chastised him about selling his career for $150,000 down the river. Don later changed his mind. "I was mistaken. Some things are intangible, and Rock adored that house and had to have it." Universal paid $167,000 to Sam Jaffe for the mansion and transferred it to Rock five years later. (It was valued at $3 million in 1985.) Rock sold his boat and transferred ownership of his Newport Beach home to his mother and Joe Olson.

Rock began a restoration and building effort that would last twenty-three years and cost more than $500,000. Rock did not declare the house finished until he was nearing the end of his life. "When the house was done, so was the man," says Mark Miller.

When he first started working on the project, Rock hired a designer and purchased books on Mexican colonial architecture, which he dubbed "the Bibles." Many of his ideas were inspired by homes in Mexico and the Southwest, such as stone archways, hand-painted tiles, and ceilings formed of whole tree limbs put on the diagonal. Rock preferred things that were dark, hefty, and enormous. He decorated the mansion with zebra skins and African masks, Spanish wooden doors, four-foot-tall pewter candlesticks, marble fireplaces, and wrought-iron candelabra. He adored massive eagle, lion, and horse statues, and his favorite color was red. His taste was reportedly described by a friend as "early Butch." "Do you ever worry about the gay part of you showing?" said Mark Miller of Rock's performance.

"There's a little girl in me that I just trample to death," Rock remarked. With his foot, he squashed something. "You will not come out!"

Rock built an environment, a world all his own, in which he would be the sole star. By day, the house feels dark and gloomy, like a medieval Spanish fortress inhabited by heavy spirits. The mansion, however, transforms into a fantasy at night. With blazing fireplaces in every room and big candles flickering in parchment shades, it's warm and inviting. The crimson rugs and candle flames are reflected in the ceiling, bringing out the wood's pink tones. Rock planned the mansion to be dubbed "Whiskey Hill," but it had a mind of its own and quickly became known as "the Castle" or "the Crest."

The rooms and every aspect of the grounds were given nicknames by Rock. There was "Assignment Lane," a zigzagged path down the cliff amid lush ferns and blossoming trees. The route could be illuminated, but Rock would leave it unlit during a party so that individuals may have "assignments" there. He dubbed the theater "the playroom," and the guest bedroom "Tijuana," because it was all red and looked like a Mexican brothel. He had a cabinet named "Texas" and a table named "Portugal." There were tropical plants and ginger in "Panama," and a plant that Rock built the outdoor urinal in "Ferndell," beside the pool. "Every good garden should have one," stated Rock. He built a greenhouse and filled it with orchids; in other areas, he grew mint for mint juleps, limes for cold daiquiris, and peaches for fresh peach ice cream, which he produced every summer ritualistically. There were terraces for corn, squash, and tomatoes, as well as cutting beds for a rainbow of tulips, zinnias, and roses.

Working in the garden with Clarence Morimoto, the full-time gardener he'd inherited from Sam Jaffe, was Rock's favorite pastime. Clarence was dubbed "the inscrutable one" by Rock because he expressed himself in a haiku-like manner.

Rock spent the majority of his time in his bedroom, kitchen, and "playroom," which he made out of what was once the garage. He furnished the playroom with the most up-to-date technological gadgets, including a jukebox, a player piano, four VCRs, audio equipment, a large-screen television, a film projector, and a film vault containing a great library of films. He possessed an entire wall of records, including rare 78s that were all numbered and categorized. There was a full bar with stools and a wooden stage with footlights where Rock practiced roles and occasionally performed shows with his pals.

In 1962, the year Rock bought his house, a young man named Lee Garlington was working as an extra on The Virginian, a television show being shot at Universal. Lee had moved to California the previous year from Atlanta, where he had grown up in a rich, conservative household. He'd joined the army and returned with a flattop and a desire to be an actor. "Once I hit town, that was it," Lee explains. "There was no way I was going to be anywhere but right in the heart of Hollywood." It was so homosexual! It was quite thrilling since there were pubs and people walking up and down the street. All you had to do, I thought, was be pretty and you'd get discovered like Rock Hudson." Lee got a job as an extra at Universal after hearing that Rock was filming Man's Favorite Sport. "I'd heard a lot about this dude. He was constantly talked about in the LGBT subculture-- how he was gay and very gorgeous and a pleasant, well-liked person. So I made the decision, "By golly, I'm going to see this man."

Lee overcame his nervousness once Rock started meeting him many times a week. Lee would drive up to the Castle after work in his 1963 Chevy Nova, sleep there, and then get back in his car and let it roll down the hill so Joy and the neighbors wouldn't find out. But Joy was aware. "You weren't pulling any wool over my eyes," she informed Lee years later.

Rock and Lee become the most important people in each other's lives. Lee desired to live with Rock, but "that was not an option." He was concerned about his image, but I would have rushed in." Lee's independence impressed Rock. He was working hard to become a broker, he never asked Rock for anything, and he insisted on paying his own way when they traveled together.

Rock and Lee took a journey around the South in 1964. Rock was concerned that the Studio could object if they found out he was traveling with another man, so in a drunken fit, he claimed he would go to the head of the Studio and tell him, "I'm gay, I have a lover, and if you don't like it, shove it up your ass."

"No way are you going to do that!" Lee stated. When Rock had calmed down, he planned to depart silently with Lee and not inform anyone. They traveled to New Orleans in first class since Lee was paying. "I can't afford first class," Lee explained to Rock. I know that's what you're used to, but all I have is tourist class, and that's hardly enough." "Okay, fine," Rock responded, and sat with Lee in the tourist section.

Before he died, Rock told Mark Miller that Lee Garlington was one of the persons he truly loved in his life. When I told Lee this, he burst into tears. He was forced to cover his face. He hadn't seen Rock since 1973 and had been unable to reach him since learning he had AIDS.I was frozen out once Rock and Tom Clark got acquainted. I never heard a nasty word from Rock, but Tom gave me the impression that I wasn't welcome. I was told that Rock had been so upset by me that I no longer had the right to be his buddy. I was embarrassed because it was my fault, and I just sort of faded out of the scene." Lee expressed regret for not being more mature when he knew Rock. "I didn't have the foresight to recognize what a wonderful man he was and to persevere." We'd probably be living together now if I'd been older and wiser."

After fourteen years with Henry Willson, Rock mustered the courage to leave and change agencies in 1962. He had been dissatisfied with Henry for many years, but had remained out of devotion and dread of Henry's reaction. Henry was not actively pursuing suitable opportunities or developing ideas for Rock. "He sat back and waited for the phone to ring," explained Rock. Rock signed with C.M.A.'s John Foreman, who described him as "virtually unknown around town." No one knew who he was, and casting directors weren't considering him. He didn't go out or entertain much. Henry Willson was uninterested in hustling, although I was."

Rock began to mingle with John and his wife, Linda, a pleasant and articulate woman from Fontana, California. They had a sparkling group of friends who saw each other all the time. "Hollywood was much more social back then." Linda describes the community as "smaller and more intimate." "John and I gave two or three parties per month." At one of their dinner parties, the group, which included Rock, imagined a small town called Newton in the "mid-USA." They made up identities, careers, and personal histories for each other. Russell Burgess, a dirt farmer, was Rock. Vi and Art Wilkins, who sold ladies' shoes, were Linda and John. Leon and Rosita Brown, Jr. (he was the town mechanic) were Steve and Neile McQueen. Lloyd Potts, a mailman, was played by Henry Fonda. Princess Grace was Olga Brooker, a ballet, adagio, and tap-toe instructor. Natalie Wood played Mary Frances Peterman, an usherette at the local cinema where Paul Newman worked as the projectionist. Helen Smeader, a beautician, was played by Faye Dunaway. Roddy McDowall played Homer Box, a CPA who lived above the theater with his mother and was madly in love with Mary Frances Peterman.

Rock was a fading breed: a studio-created movie star marketed by fan magazines, whose looks were initially more important than his acting talent. He had no resemblance to a living being. "How could he suddenly play a smaller-than-life, utterly realistic figure?"

According to John Foreman. "You can't imagine Rock Hudson and Al Pacino coexisting on the same planet, let alone in the same film." Rock actively despised politics during these years of social and political change in the country. He considered himself a patriotic American and voted Republican. But he would never participate in a political debate, let alone a movement. He never endorsed politicians or attended festivities, and he never contributed to a campaign. He was perplexed as he watched the Vietnam protests and civic instability on television. The only time he was directly involved was during the Watts riots in 1965.

On that July night in 1965, Rock stood on the porch with Joy, watching the smoke rise up over the ghetto, where blacks were looting and setting fires while police and residents were engaged in gun battles. Joy was concerned about Peggy, her best friend who lived in Watts. She called Peggy and discovered she had no electricity, limited food, and had barricaded herself in. "Tell her we're coming," Rock said. Joy thought it was a ridiculous notion, and she was afraid a sniper would take them out. But Rock climbed into the back of his new Chrysler Town & Country station wagon and started the engine. Joy and her son, Gil, got in their car, "and we hit the freeway," Joy adds.

Rock drove around police roadblocks and through buildings that appeared to be bombed-out ruins. "We passed police officers in riot gear and kids holding rocks and Molotov cocktails, and I kept expecting one to fly through the window." We were in a big glossy automobile, with a white man, a black woman, a child, and a German shepherd that may have been an attack dog. If that didn't look funny on Central Avenue." Rock went on to make less and less successful comedies: Strange Bedfellows, A Very Special Favor, Blindfold. He had a close group of crew members with whom he had worked for years and who he now insisted on hiring for every film he did. They were known as "the bridge group" because they would play bridge with Rock in between setups. Rock had become an adept player after the fiasco in 1951, when he attempted to study bridge from Mark Miller and fell with laughter. Mark Reedall, his makeup artist, Pete Saldutti, his wardrobe guy, and George Robotham, his stuntman and double, were all with him all the while. The group ate together, drank together, went on trips together, and were constantly trying to "hang each other" with puns and practical jokes.

Rock gave him a look. "Jesus Christ, Bernie. "I was only joking."
Bernie's face sagged. "Kidding. "What will I tell my parents?"
Rock felt terrible as Bernie fell out of the trailer. When Mark came in
to touch up his makeup, he had picked up needlepoint and was
working on a pillow. Rock informed him of what had occurred with
Bernie.
"Yeah, Rock," Mark confirmed. "I put him up to it."
For the longest period, Rock sewed without saying anything. Mark
kept an eye on him. "I just knew I had him." Rock jerked his head up
and smacked his work on the table. "Fuck you fuck you fuck you
fuck you!"
The gags became more intricate and serious until everyone realized
the game was "getting too strong" and decided to stop.
After seven years at the top, Rock fell to second place in the Motion
Picture Film Buyers' poll as a "Name Power Star" in 1964. In 1965,
he fell to tenth place, where he remained in 1966. Then, in 1967, he
dropped completely off the charts.
The irony was that Rock was hitting his stride as an actor at the same
time he was losing popularity. In 1966, he starred in Seconds, which
showcased a depth and brilliance in his acting that he'd never had the
chance to showcase before. It wasn't a romance or a comedy, but
rather a gloomy, cautionary narrative.
Seconds, which was recently released, is the most recent film I'm
excited about. As controversial as he/1--a weird... terrifying horror
picture. I play a sixty-year-old man who has been "reborn." I've had a
facelift, and there's a before and after, with me being the "after" for
most of the photo. They linked it to the Faust narrative at the Cannes
Film Festival.
Rock plays a banker in the eastern suburbs who is locked in a
loveless marriage and a suffocating life in Seconds. He visits a
mystery "clinic," where he is sold a new life. They operate on him,
give him a new face and body, even a new voice, stage a fake
"death" for his old self, and place him in Malibu as a painter with a
house and studio on the beach, new acquaintances, and even a
mistress. "You've got what every middle-aged man in America
would like," the clinic director says. "Freedom." Rock does not
adjust well to his new life; the annihilation of his past and all of its
associations has left him feeling disoriented. When he realizes that

43

his new friends and lover are also "reborns," he revolts and returns to the clinic to reclaim his old life.

The film handed Rock his most difficult role to date. He had to transform himself from an uptight businessman who was cautious and dour to a free spirit who could strip naked and stomp bare in a vat of grapes, laughing and losing himself in Dionysian abandon. Then he had to become a rage-filled soul, desperate for a feeble and unattainable chance to relive his life on his own terms.

John Frankenheimer directed the picture, which was shot in black-and-white by James Wong Howe. Many of the photos were warped, as if seen through a fish-eye lens, giving it an uncanny aesthetic character. Rock only drank on the job for seconds. At a party, he had a long intoxicated incident in which he had to have an emotional outburst and collapse. He wasn't sure how to play it, so he stayed intoxicated for three days while they shot the sequence, with Frankenheimer's approval. Rock's conversation coach, Jimmy Dobson, fought against it. "I think the best drunk scenes are played by people who don't drink," adds Dobson. "But because the scene turned out so well, I had a hard time convincing Rock that this was not the way to go."

In the spring of 1966, the film was exhibited at the Cannes Film Festival. Rock stopped in Hamburg to see Mark Miller and George Nader, who had gone to Germany in 1964 after George signed a contract to create eleven films in which he portrayed Jerry Cotton, a kind of German James Bond. Rock greeted Mark and George at the airport, and as they drove back to town, Rock stated, "I want to tell you something right away." "I am now a world-famous celebrity."

They were perplexed by his appearance. "Good. Very good."

"I'm serious, you guys. "I'm a global celebrity."

"Wonderful," said George. "How was it on your flight?"

When Mark and George were alone, they wondered what had become of Rock. "We knew he was a global superstar. He presented the news as if it were the word of God, chiseled in stone from the mountain. It was difficult to bear. This was the man we used to buy dinner for with the money Mark earned at the drive-in. We'd gone too far back and seen too much for him to pull this."

Rock and Mark proceeded to separate parties before meeting at the Carlton Hotel at four a.m.

"Shit," said Rock. "I thought I'd had a hit."

Mark stated that the opening half hour of the film, prior to the appearance of Rock, was boring and dull. "It's going to kill you." "Can't you convince them to reshoot it?" That was not conceivable, according to Rock. The picture was released in the United States and swiftly vanished. However, it developed a cult following over time, and Rock began to receive honors and accolades from film clubs and institutions. Rock eventually learned to like it again and consider it among his best work.

In the summer of 1966, Rock canceled his contract with Universal and became, for the first time, a free agent, free to produce films anywhere he wanted and chose the roles he wanted rather than those given by the studio. But his most recent flicks had been flops, and he found himself dressed up and with nowhere to go. There were no offers on the phone. Rock became depressed; he had grown accustomed to working constantly. Was the thrilling trip over?

It was around this time that Rock emerged from the "impossible stage" and reverted to the Rock Hudson that his old friends remembered. "He came down off his high horse," George Nader remembers, "just in time to jump into the bottle." Every night, Rock began to drink heavily. He would not eat until ten or eleven o'clock because he needed another Scotch and soda and refused to drink after eating. When he invited people to dinner, they'd start hints and then ask for food, but Rock would answer, "Oh, let's have another drink." "If you're invited here for dinner, you better eat first," Joy advised. When asked why Rock was drinking so much, Tom Clark replied, "He can't stand it that he's no longer number one."

Rock was getting friends with Tom Clark, a publicist at M.G.M. They met during a bridge game in 1964, and Rock began having dinners with Tom and his longtime companion, Pete De Palma. Rock traveled to the Far East with De Palma shortly after leaving Universal, and while in Hong Kong, he received a distressing call from his business manager, Andy Maree. Rock had little understanding of finance and had no desire to learn; he left all financial decisions to Maree. When Maree told him, "You're down to fifteen hundred dollars in the bank," he was taken aback. You should go home and go to work."

Tom Clark informed Rock that Martin Ransohoff was working on a film called Ice Station Zebra at M.G.M.

"God, I'd love to do that," remarked Rock.

"Why don't you come out to the studio and have lunch with me, then walk into Marty's office and say, 'Hi, my name is Rock Hudson, and I'd like to do Ice Station Zebra,'" she suggests. Rock heeded Tom's advice, his agent campaigned, and when Laurence Harvey dropped out of the lead role, Rock stepped in.

The film provided Rock a boost--he was still a star--and he showed a youthful enthusiasm for the technical parts of the production: the icebergs, snowstorms, and the nuclear submarine built on the sound stage. Tom Clark was tasked with doing publicity for the picture, and it was the first time he and Rock collaborated.

In 1967, while filming the film, Rock met an eccentric young man who would prove Rock's match for foolishness and chuckling. He'd be the first guy to live with Rock since 1954, and the Castle would erupt with laughter and fun.

Chapter 5

Frank Shea, who owned the former Dick Powell and Joan Blondell mansion in Beverly Hills and had a tennis court that was always open to anyone, was a friend of Rock's. In the summer of 1967, Rock dropped by to hit balls and socialize. He had left his racket there by accident, and when he returned to recover it, there was a new group of players on the court. Rock met a young man named Jack Coates, who was twenty-three and extremely attractive: tanned, blond, and sun-washed. But he was more than just a good-looking guy. He had a glimmer in his eye and a restless energy that made him appear electrified and alive. Rock shook hands and walked off the court, then stopped beyond the ivy-covered gate. There were a few openings in the ivy, and Rock positioned himself near one to watch the game unnoticed.

The only celebrity he wished to meet was Rock Hudson. He began driving by Rock's house on his route to and from courses after the day at the tennis court, when "I noticed I was noticed," he claimed. The Corvette broke down in front of the home one day. Jack had opened the hood and was repairing the problem when Rock appeared with one of his dogs. "Hello!" he said. "Do you require assistance?" "The strongest impression I have of Rock is the way he said, 'Hi!'" recounts Jack. It was so deep and hearty that it would lasso you into a warm nice feeling. 'Hi!'" Jack had hoped for something like this to happen, but when he saw Rock approaching him, he became terrified, closed the hood, and drove away. A few days later, he was driving down a narrow, winding road in the hills when he noticed Rock, in a blue Cadillac convertible, in front of him. When Rock noticed the Corvette in his rearview mirror, he pulled over and blocked the street. "Hi! "Would you like to go out to lunch?"

"I can't, I have to get to work," Jack explained.

"Where?" "Standard Oil, Wilshire and La Cienega.""

Rock came into the gas station in the blue Cadillac and pulled alongside Jack. "Fill her right up." The car used a gallon and a half of gas. Rock returned an hour later with the Chrysler station wagon. "Fill her up," he ordered, and three gallons were required. He inquired as to what time Jack left work.

"I leave at ten o'clock tonight."

"Why don't you come on by for a steam or a swim?"

They began playing "a cat and mouse game," in which Rock pursued Jack and Jack would let himself get captured and then leap off. He'd slip out to see Rock, then withdraw to his home with the developer and refuse to answer Rock's phone calls. Mark Miller flew in from Europe to file his taxes that summer, and when he arrived at the Castle, Rock remarked, "I've found him I " He clutched his shirt over his heart, causing it to flutter, while rolling his gaze skyward. "He's dynamite, but someone else has him, so it'll take time." Rock hosted a thirty-person party for Mark, and Mark noticed a blond in tennis gear with naughty blue eyes and "gorgeous legs." His entire person appeared to sparkle." Mark approached him and grinned. "You're brand new."

Jack Coates had been with the developer for five years and was hesitant to leave. People told him that Rock would utilize and then discard him. "I can't see you anymore, I'm happy where I am," Jack said to Rock. But Rock kept calling, sometimes from his Cadillac, which was parked on the hill above Jack's house.

"Look, I like you more than I ever loved anybody," Jack said.

"Let's go to Will Wright's and have double-vanilla ice cream with extra hot-fudge sauce," Rock proposed.

"People say you're not sincere," Jack pointed out.

"Let's go to Bob's Big Boy and get outside trays before ordering cheeseburgers with extra catsup."

Jack quickly became popular among Rock's buddies. Tom Clark and Pete De Palma taught him how to play bridge, and when Rock was on location, Jack would join Tom and Pete. Mark and George saw Jack as a free spirit with whom Rock might rediscover his childish delight in the outrageous. "Everyone fell in love with Jack at first sight," Mark explains. "He's outgoing and bright, and his eyes sparkle with delight." "He makes you want to laugh." Jack couldn't sit still, and when he spoke, he used his entire body, bending his knees, gesticulating with his arms, and flinging his head back. "Can that cat dance!" exclaimed Joy. "Every single muscle in his body is tense." He operated on his own timetable and was difficult to locate. "You have to nail him when you get him-two spikes to the ground," one of his friends advised. He was a young man in the 1960s who was inspired by youth culture. He donned pants and a Navajo Indian buckle, became a vegetarian, and used marijuana, which Rock tried but did not like. Rock thought cocaine was "terrible-sobered me right up," and requested that no one smoke or use illegal narcotics in the house.

Rock's wordplay and games piqued Jack's interest. Rock was constantly looking up word origins and inventing jokes. "Why do people say 'There, there!' when consoling someone and 'Here, here!' when reprimanding someone?" Rock once questioned Jack. Rock referred to Jack as a "bad doggie." "What's the worst thing on the planet?" Jack asks. "He's a bad dog." When something went wrong in the house, Rock pointed to Jack and said, "Bad doggie." Rock had nicknames for everything: Tijuana for the guest bedroom and "the Narrows" for the back road down to Sunset, which reminded Rock of a perilous strait.

They didn't talk about how Jack's move may harm Rock's career, but Jack believed he should be cautious in public. If they went to a concert or a big event, they went separately, and Jack avoided taking pictures. "It wasn't so much a deception," Jack explains, "as it was a role." Rock was an actor who took on two parts: one in public and one at home. He was reserved in public, but at home, he could be what he called a "secret libertine."

Except for Joy, the seven dogs, and Clarence, Rock and Jack had the entire house to themselves. "The dogs ran wild, went in the pool with us, and ate out of the same dish," Jack explains. Rock had a story and a nickname for each of the dogs. Fritz, or "Fritz the Nitz," a German shepherd, was his first and most adored pet. Miss Sally was a huge, white Belgian shepherd, and her daughter, Wee Wee, was the runt of the litter that Rock had helped Sally deliver in the rain outside the kitchen while wearing a tuxedo after a premiere. Another German shepherd was Nick the Dumb. Mr. Murphy was a schnauzer gifted to Rock by admirers, while Jack and Jill were Irish setters given the names Rhett and Scarlett from Gone With the Wind.

In the summer, Rock and Jack enjoyed lying by the pool and swimming. Because there was no diving board in the pool, Rock devised a game called "underwater slow-motion diving." He'd try a four and a half gainer under water before running out of breath, but one of the dogs would generally go down and try to pull him up by his trunks, while the other dogs growled.

Rock and Jack also enjoyed playing hide-and-seek. Jack would climb one of the trees, and if Rock took too long to find him, he'd send the dogs after him, yelling, "Unfair!" They both enjoyed working in the garden with Clarence. They'd bring the radio and stools into the greenhouse and sit for hours potting and repotting plants. "Our favorite tree was the star pine," Jack describes. It was a Norfolk Island pine with five branches on each tier, arranged in the shape of a star. They were competing to see who could spot the most star pines. Rock once telegraphed Jack, "Saw a star pine yesterday, in Rome."

Jack assisted Rock in remodeling the house. "Let's go down to Meade Wrecking in Pasadena and see if they have anything interesting," Rock would suggest. They drove down to the wrecking yard, where Rock discovered a set of fake Greek columns that had originally been in front of a bank. He had the columns brought to the Castle and arranged for them to be set around the pool. He also discovered a massive marble fireplace, which he put in the formal living room. "People told him it was too enormous and wouldn't draw--it had been an ornamental piece in an old mansion's ballroom-- but Rock bought it and it worked perfectly."

They liked to plan barbecues on weekends. They'd rent a dozen old movies to play in the playroom indefinitely, and they'd buy two inch-thick steaks and marinate them in bourbon and teriyaki sauce. Rock still preferred to grill the steaks himself and has yet to provide an edible piece of meat. Rock's eating habits struck Jack as odd. "For a late-night snack, he liked peanut butter and jelly, ham and cheese, and Miracle Whip on white bread." He ate uncooked hamburger from the packet with his fingers and was always begging for gizzards. 'Joy, could you make a pot of gizzies?' "

The years Rock spent with Jack were joyful ones, full of good moments and stability, with minimal conflict. Jack claims he and Rock never argued or disagreed. "If something bothered him, he wouldn't talk about it, he'd get silent, but his silence was more devastating than anyone's anger because you could feel it all through the house." "What's wrong?" Joy would inquire of Jack. "Did you do anything?"

"No, didn't you?" Jack stated.

"Perhaps it's something at the studio," Joy suggested, and they'd sit down in the kitchen to figure it out. "But the silence never lasted more than a day," Jack explains.

"Rock wasn't introspective, and he didn't talk about his feelings, but we could communicate in an unusual way." They sat and peered into one other's eyes without saying anything. "It made other people nervous if they were around, but for me, it was bliss."

Rock traveled to Europe in the spring of 1968 to film Darling Lili with Julie Andrews. The picture was behind time and over budget when Rock arrived, and the environment was frantic. Rock informed Jack that he had previously met Julie, and that when he performed his first scene with her, she told him, "You realize, I'm a big star now." Rock smiled as he started a cigarette. "We appreciate your joining us."

Rock summoned Jack Coates, who had never traveled to Europe before. It was the first time Rock had a lover visit him on set, and he gave Jack two airline tickets so he could travel with another man, a gay international banker. It appears that Jack was the banker's friend rather than Rock's. "I stayed up all night on the plane because I was so excited to go to Paris, France, and Europe," Jack says. It was exhilarating for Rock to take someone he cared about to a location he'd never been before. He escorted Jack to the Cafe Foch for wild raspberries and heavy cream, then to the Eiffel Tower, where Rock had a special pass to go up on a private viewing deck. "I tried to be cool," Jack adds. "I leaned against the railing and exclaimed, 'So this is Paris.'"

Jack slept all day the next day, and when he awoke, Rock was dressed and ready for dinner. "How come you let me sleep inl?"

"We know what's best for you," Rock winked. "This is the city of Paris."

Rock joined Jack at the Castle for the summer after he stayed for three weeks to finish the film. "Let's have some fun in the sun with Dick and Jane," remarked Rock.

The summer of 1968 was the most volatile of the decade, with two recent assassinations, violent anti-Vietnam War protests, and a Democratic National Convention conducted behind barbed wire. "What is this crap?" muttered Rock as he watched the news on television. Let us rejoice in America." He didn't understand the protests, just as he wouldn't grasp the homosexual rights movement a few years later, "where you march with a jar of Vaseline." He couldn't understand why people would force their religious or sexual ideas on others. But he didn't dwell on the news. "He was too busy showing old movies and barbecuing," Jack explains.

Rock hosted "the last great Hollywood party" for Carol Burnett, according to many. Carol Burnett's television shows had included Rock, and the two had become great friends. Rock had been encouraged to entertain by John and Linda Foreman because his house was great for parties and few people in the Hollywood community had been there. When he hosted Carol's party, "everyone came." Rock and his team spent weeks planning. They drained the pool, erected scaffolding over it, and installed a parquet dance floor. Clarence tied flower chains around the outdoor columns and scattered flowering plants throughout the patio. A mariachi band was hired to roam the grounds and play Mexican tunes, while an orchestra was contracted to perform near the dance floor.

When Barbra Streisand stepped in, Jack Coates was seated with Jack Benny. She'd just made her cinematic debut in Funny Girl, and everyone was craning their necks to catch a glimpse of her. "Look, there's Barbra Streisand," Jack Benny pointed out.

"But you're Jack Benny," said Jack Coates.

The last guests had left around six o'clock in the morning. Rock sat at the bar with Jack Coates and Joy, one hand holding a Scotch and soda, the other a cigarette.

"Isn't it beautiful?" remarked Rock.

"It's gorgeous," Joy exclaimed.

"What are we gonna do with all these flowers?" Jack stated.

Joy advised that they retire to bed.

"Good idea," remarked Rock. But they were all immobile, relishing the aftertaste of a long and spectacular night. Snippets of discussion, unforgettable faces, amusing gestures and exchanges, glistening hair, and the sound of trumpets raced through their heads.

Jack wondered, "How did I get here?" Why am I so lucky?

Ice Station Zebra premiered at the Cinerama Dome in Hollywood in October 1968. Rock chose Flo Allen, a beautiful woman who had become his agent once John Foreman began producing pictures. Someone in the throng yelled, "Faggot!" as Rock exited the limousine. Rock turned white and wanted to plow through the crowd in search of the heckler. Tom Clark, who was nearby, grabbed Rock's arm and led him to where columnist Army Archerd was conducting live television interviews. Rock exited the theater using a side door after the interview. "That's all there is to it! "I'll never go to another premiere," he declared.

In 1969, Rock traveled to Durango, Mexico, to work on The Undefeated, a western starring John Wayne. He'd never worked with Wayne before and was apprehensive about meeting the man who personified America's ideal of macho strength. Wayne was putting natural lipstick in a little mirror when Rock first noticed him on set. Wayne squinted his eyes at Rock as they were introduced. "Well," he sighed, "I hear you're a good bridge player."

Wayne began making suggestions to me on the first day of shooting. "Why don't you just turn your head this way...?" as well as "Why don't you hold your gun like that for a close shot?" They sounded like fantastic ideas, so I tried them, but that night I began to wonder whether I was going to be directed by this guy. Is he attempting to assert dominance or something? So I told him the next day, "Why don't you turn your head this way...?"

Rock returned home for a few months before heading to Italy to work on The Hornet's Nest with Sylva Koscina. He'd been promised that Sophia Loren would be his co-star, but Koscina had been called in at the last minute. Rock sent Jack amusing letters. "This is my new Italian secretary (who is actually a portable Olivetti)." She can't spell and you have to press her quite hard, but she's a faithful girl." Rock noted that he liked the picture and that one of the young lads in the cast had "great natural talent." Rock was never able to determine whether a film was succeeding while filming it, but by engaging himself in the character, he became emotionally committed, and inevitably he was imbued with hope.

He was frequently let down, as he was with The Hornet's Nest. Rock arrived at the Castle in time for Christmas, and his job and business anxieties faded.

Rock had always made it a condition of his contracts that he have the last few weeks of December free to devote to Christmas. Christmas was the pinnacle of the Rock year, when music, laughter, food, and drink, as well as the delight of surprising people with inventive and welcoming gifts, all came together in one beautiful celebration. When asked for a one-word explanation of Rock, Roger Jones said, "Christmas." Consider the music, the color, the lights, and everything else that Christmas may signify to different people--this was Rock."

Rock and Jack went down to the railroad yard to see the first Christmas trees unloaded from the boxcars. They waited for Rock to spot "the perfect tree." It was about twelve feet tall and was placed in the stairs between the formal living room and the "red room," which had a crimson rug and the huge couches from the set of Pillow Talk. Rock and Jack went to the downtown flower market next, where they bought pine boughs, mistletoe, wreaths, and pots of scarlet poinsettias, which Rock referred to as "apointasettas." The house would be filled with the aroma of pine.

Rock went out and bought gifts for everyone on his list, wrapped them, and delivered them himself. He'd worked as a gift wrapper in Chicago one Christmas and turned the playroom into a wrapping station. He sat for hours, surrounded by skeins of various colored ribbons, rolls of paper, pinecones, and baubles.

Rock used to wander around Universal Studios with a large burlap sack, delivering presents. Each present demonstrated thinking and planning. Gail Gifford adored a set of stools in Rock's home and got them for Christmas. Jack Coates had said in passing that he wanted to learn to ski, so his gift was a hole ski outfit, including metal skis, boots and poles, pants, sweaters, coats, socks, long underwear, caps, gloves, and goggles, as well as a ski trip and lessons. Rock gifted his mother a diamond necklace, an organ, and a world cruise one year.

Joy had spent a week preparing for the Christmas Day feast. She requested a freshly slaughtered turkey and two pounds of additional gizzards. She shined the silver and transformed the crimson room into a dining room. The couches were moved aside and a huge table with a linen cover and silver candelabra with giant red candles was erected in their place. The centerpiece included crystal and silver goblets, as well as boughs and berries. Joy took photographs when it was ready, which she would proudly display years later. "That was my dining table."

Rock put on his Christmas music and made his regular eggnog around 5 p.m. on Christmas Day. "What a mess in the kitchen," comments Joy. "That eggnog was so potent that it could have walked out there on its own." 'Joy, want a glass?' Rock would ask. 'You want dinner?' I'd ask.

Rock's mother, Kay, drove over from Newport Beach with baked pies, as did Mark and George, who came in from Europe, as did Lynn Bowers and Pat Fitzgerald, Tom Clark and Pete De Palma, and Peter Shore, the decorator who worked on the house with Rock. Rock wore corduroy pants and a bright red shirt most of the time. Jim Nabors arrived in a candy-apple-red Rolls-Royce convertible, sporting a Blackglama mink coat, one Christmas. "Do you think Jim has gone to Hollywood?" Rock asked, leaning very close to Jack Coates.

Joy sliced the turkey with dressing and cranberries, ham, corn pudding, handmade relishes and buns, three veggies, and at least three varieties of pie. Rock talked about his mother's pumpkin pie and how she cooked it from scratch, harvesting and cooking the pumpkins herself. Kay walked to the kitchen when he finished eating and returned with a box from the bakery company Marie Callender's. The rock's face collapsed. Everyone laughed, but Kay flung the box into the fireplace and winked, "I just had that box from an old bridge party."

Rock gave his gifts after supper. He disliked receiving things and frequently gave them away, but he enjoyed watching his friends open their gifts from him. More music was played by Rock, and people gathered around the Steinway grand piano to sing. Rock would return to the kitchen late at night, when everyone had left, and eat a platter of gizzards with Joy's turkey gravy. No one who spent a Christmas with Rock ever had another experience like it, not because the ingredients were unique, but because it meant so much to Rock.

Pretty Maids All in a Row, an X-rated black comedy directed by Roger Vadim, a famed sensualist who was then married to Jane Fonda, gave Rock his first opportunity to play a villain in 1970. "I'm a killer and a stud!" "I get to do it all," Rock said Mark Miller. Tiger, a high-school counselor, screwed the prettiest ladies in school and murdered them when they became difficult, played by Rock. Rock, as Tiger, has a mustache, wears hip-hugger jeans, and enjoys balancing on a bongo board. He appears to have a perpetual hard-on and needs to keep the girls away from him. The video evokes the essence of a time when sex was prevalent and everyone wanted to try it on everyone else. The females dress in miniskirts and see-through shirts, flaunting their bouncing breasts, wiggling rears, and long, exposed legs. Angie Dickinson plays a sex-deprived teacher, and in one scene, Rock takes up her blouse and grabs her breasts with both hands, forces her down on the table, climbs on top of her, and then pauses and leaves her clawing. The picture is a muddled mash-up of parody and murder mystery that doesn't work, but Rock's sexual thrill is evident and puts the viewer in a state of excitement. The

Chicago Sun Times reviewer Roger Ebert observed, "Rock Hudson sex comedies sure have changed since Pillow Talk."

Rock was about to enter a phase in which sex would be his primary concern. He told his pals that he needed to have sex every day and that he was always thinking about it. He was thinking about having sex that night throughout business meetings and while traveling in the car. He informed Mark Miller that he cared about three things in this order: sex, career, and people. According to Jack Coates, when Rock strolled into a gathering, "the entire room filled with sexual heat." It was felt by both men and women. He was that powerful. 'Wanna have some fun?' was his favorite expression. You already knew what that meant."

Rock, according to Jack, preferred blue or white linens and down pillows on his bed. He was known as the "champion cuddler." "They're having cuddling championships this year in Davos, Switzerland," he once wrote to Jack from Europe. It's possible to ski from Davos to Klosters and stay at inns along the way, although it's really cold. Let's enter; I believe we can win."

It was around this time when the first public questions about Rock's sexual orientation were raised. In the summer of 1971, a group of gay men in Manhattan Beach, California, who held a party with a hilarious theme every year, sent out invitations to a party commemorating Rock Hudson and Jim Nabors' wedding. One of the cards ended up in the hands of a gossip columnist, who published an article in which he did not name names but stated that two male Hollywood stars had married. "One is like the Rock of Gibraltar; the other is like your next-door neighbor."

The idea grew that Rock Hudson had secretly married Jim Nabors. It was repeated on television and radio shows, as well as in numerous columns, and the Castle's phone was continuously ringing with reporters seeking response. There was no truth to it; Rock had appeared on Jim Nabors' variety show as a guest, and they had become casual acquaintances. Rock enjoyed singing with Jim, and he and Jack Coates had traveled to Lake Tahoe to ski and witness Jim's performance. When Jim's house burned down, Rock called and said, "You can stay here, you can wear our underwear," but Jim never came to the Castle. When Joy heard the rumor, she told Rock, "Of course it's not true." He isn't even blonde."

Rock initially disregarded it, believing that if he refused to deal with an uncomfortable situation, he could will it away. When he did speak up, he made a joke about it, telling Joyce Haber, "It's over. I've returned all of Jim's emeralds and diamonds." Finally, both Rock and Jim were forced to make public comments stating that the wedding did not take place. Rona Barrett stated on her TV show Rona Reporm in July that "We've received thousands of calls and letters from across the country inquiring about the veracity of perhaps Hollywood's most vicious rumor in the last fifty years." We unequivocally state that the wedding never took place. This heinous rumor is completely false.``

Rock grew enraged; how could he defend himself when everyone was saying that something false had occurred? Jim Nabors' CBS variety program was canceled, and he and Rock were never seen together again. Rock was even hesitant to visit Hawaii because he knew Jim owned property there. They didn't say anything for the remainder of Rock's life.Jack informed Rock two days before Christmas in 1971 that he had decided to return to Arizona. "Rock would not show any emotion," Jack observes, "he was silent." Jack sobbed his way down the steps, into his truck, and drove away. Joy asked, "What happened?" to Mark Miller.

Rock could have stopped Jack from leaving if he had wanted to, but he said nothing and let him walk out. They communicated on the phone, and Jack returned frequently for trips and holidays. "Jack was like a knight," adds Mark. "Whenever he wanted, he could seize the movie star and take him away, and nobody could do anything."

Jack traveled the Southwest with his pickup truck, visiting Indian reservations and meditation centers. Rock never discussed their relationship with Jack until many years later, after Rock's mother died and Rock ran into Jack in Santa Fe, New Mexico. They desired alone, so they trekked up a trail in the Sangre de Cristo Mountains, and while they stood in a clearing, chatting softly, Rock asked Jack, "What went wrong?"

Chapter 6

For many years, Rock had been contacted about doing television, but he had never seriously considered it. He considered television to be a lower form, a haven for sinking ships that couldn't float in the broad sea. He had chastised George Nader for doing television in the 1950s, despite the fact that he did not even watch television. He had always wanted to work in film.

However, Rock was a romantic leading man, not a character actor, and there were fewer romantic leads for him in 1971. He was 46 years old, gaining weight, and losing skin tone as a result of his heavy drinking. It became necessary for him to have his clothing custom-made to conceal the additional flesh around his waist. Friends and advisers began to persuade him, "There's a whole other career out there for you on television, a whole new generation you could reach." The young people who had flocked to see Rock Hudson in the 1950s were now at home, raising families and watching television.

Rock contacted Leonard Stern at home after dinner and said, "Well, it has to be Susan." "I've put on seven pounds." Following Susan, they cast Nancy Walker as the household maid and John Schuck as Sergeant Enright, Rock's sidekick.

"Once Upon a Dead Man," the pilot, was shot in Rock's home, with the red room serving as the set for Rock and Susan's living room. Susan, whose straight black hair was parted in the middle and fell halfway down her back on the first day of rehearsals, was dressed in a short slip called a "teddy." Rock was seated on the couch, and she cRock and Susan had fantastic chemistry on TV, despite their twenty-year age difference. However, the relationship was unpleasant for Rock at first. Susan struck him as a flower child, a member of the antiwar generation who ate brown rice and had babies at home while nursing them on set. She was fresh to the trade and might be irritable. Rock was "Mr. Meat" to Susan. He only wanted to eat steak. He'd grown a beard and was dressed in jackets with large lapels and wide ties that I assumed were on their way out." He smoked and drank and would say, "Pack the ecology." Let us extract more oil from the ground." He was an old guard Hollywood star with a bodyguard about him. Susan was a "baby" at the time, developing an acting technique as she went, a loose, natural manner that contrasted with the tighter acting employed on television at the time. "If Susan put what she puts into rehearsal on film, she'd be a huge star," Rock told Tom Clark. But as soon as the camera starts rolling, she tightens up and doesn't display her true talent."

The show was a success and aired for six years. Despite their apparent differences, Rock and Susan eventually became excellent friends. "We were together for twelve hours a day," Susan explains. "You spend more time with your spouse than you do with me." When you're working together so closely and giving each other the energy and spark that makes it work on screen, you can't help but fall in love." Susan and her husband used to go to Rock's on Sunday nights to watch the performance and have dinner, and they were always asked on Christmas Eve.

She claims she has never seen Rock have a temper tantrum or throw his weight around. He had a contract condition that said he couldn't work late on Fridays, which everyone envied him for, but whenever he was requested to work late, he always did so without complaint.

McMillan and Wife were never enough for Rock. He kept a professional demeanor, was always prepared and on time, and was pleasant and helpful to everyone, but he never gave his all to the role. He drank every night at home, partially because he was unhappy with what he was doing. Susan was nominated for an Emmy four of the five years she hosted the show, but Rock was not.

Many showgoers had never seen Rock's flicks. They recognized him as the television figure and liked him because they saw the sensitivity beneath the macho investigator. "He was beautiful and strong, but he also seemed like a man who could be a real friend," one young woman stated. You could approach him."

Susan's contract expired at the end of the fifth season, and she demanded more money than the firm was ready to pay. She had had enough of playing the same character and was ready to move on. "I didn't realize how good I had it," she admitted later. She quit the program, and Rock played McMillan for another season.

Chapter 7

Marilyn Maxwell died of a heart attack in March 1972, and Rock was one of the first people to call. Marilyn's fifteen-year-old son, Matthew Davis, had returned home from school and saw mom slumped on the closet floor. He summoned the paramedics, who informed him, "Your mother has died." Matthew was taken aback. He entered the maid's room at the back of the home and sat in a large crimson chair. The house started to fill up, but Matthew refused to leave his chair. People were chatting to him, but he couldn't understand them and glanced around in confusion. A face appeared out of nowhere. Rock Hudson, together with Marilyn's secretary, Jean Greenberg, took Matthew in his arms, carried him out to his car, and drove him up to the Castle. Rock summoned a doctor, who administered a tranquilizer to Matthew before placing him in the Tijuana guest room.

Rock sat on the floor of the red room with Jean all night, drinking vodka straight up, answering phones, and making funeral arrangements. Rock served as a pallbearer and sat with Tom Clark and Jimmy Dobson during the service. Rock and Jimmy were trying not to cry. "Jimmy, tell me about the next picture I'm doing," Rock whispered under his breath. "How will it be?"

"You'll be in a lovely country." Tall green trees and red mountains. "Clean air that feels good to breathe."

"That's correct. "I'm going to like it," Rock predicted.

Rock turned to Tom on his way out and said he didn't want a funeral. "Please, please, please, don't ever let them do this to me."

Rock searched through Marilyn's belongings a few days later and discovered old '78 recordings of every radio broadcast she had done. He put them to tape and delivered them to Matthew. "I didn't realize how important it was to preserve those recordings until later," Matthew recalls. Rock simply knew what to do. He was my mother's best friend."

Showdown, filmed in New Mexico in 1972, was the next film Rock worked on to distract himself from the loss of Marilyn Maxwell. There was a scene in which Rock had to drive an ancient car borrowed from Laurence Rockefeller's collection. The brakes failed while Rock was practicing, and the automobile slammed into a concrete wall at full speed. Rock sustained a concussion, a shattered rib, and fractures in both legs and arms. The production was suspended, and he flew home to recover in bed for six weeks.

Mark Miller and George Nader had returned to the United States from Europe, and George had been in an accident that was even more catastrophic than Rock's. He had a detached retina and went blind in one eye. He had surgery to restore the retina, but he got glaucoma, which ended his career abruptly and unexpectedly. He couldn't work in movies since the bright lights caused him to lose his vision. When he learned about the sickness, Rock became upset. Rock was terrified of blindness and frequently stated, "I could live with anything but that." Every year, he made a donation to eye clinics and blind institutes.

When Mark and George arrived at the Castle for supper, Rock asked, "What are you gonna do now, if George can't work?" "I'm going to sell real estate," Mark declared. He'd gotten his license and a job with Larry O'Rourke Realty as a salesman.

"No, you're not," Rock responded. "You're gonna work for me."

"But...what will I do?"

"Manage my affairs. "I require the services of a secretary."

"There's nothing to do," Mark stated flatly.

The remark would become a running gag. "There's nothing for me to do."

Mark states, "It was a full-time job, and it took seven days a week if I let it." Mark established an office in Tijuana, complete with a desk and files, and took over the management of Rock's home. He handled all of the mail and phone calls, paid all of the bills, kept records, and resolved the difficulties that surrounded Rock. The house was nicknamed "Castle Chaos" by Mark because there was usually a brush fire going and Rock sat calmly while others got their hands burned trying to put it out. Rock was nine months behind on payments and had years of fan letters piling up in boxes. "The cars were a complete mess," Mark says. "Rock had six cars, but none of them had gas or oil." Rock would drive them until they ran out of gas or broke down, at which point he would switch to another vehicle."

Mark was paid $100 per week by Rock. Joy was still paid $60 per week, while Clarence had been paid $600 per month since 1962. Rock was referred to as "cheap chicken" by Mark. He was the most generous and inexpensive person I had ever met." Rock never looked for prices when he shopped, but he refused to grant raises and instructed his employees to clip coupons and shop for groceries on Thursdays, when the markets had deals. Rock gave Mark and George a vacation to Europe for Christmas, but added, "I can't afford to send you first class." I hope you don't mind going on a tourism excursion." "I took the job because it was fun," Mark says. Where else could I possibly find something like this? I worked from nine to four, had excursions to Hawaii, New York, and Europe, and got to spend the entire day sitting with my best buddy, making jokes and chuckling." Rock sat in the office in a wooden chair with lions' heads carved into the arms, which had formerly belonged to George Nader's mother. Rock needlepointed while Mark typed and messengers, workers, and barbers came and departed. He'd taken up the skill while recuperating from foot surgery. When Rock complained about being bored, Tom Clark sent him a beginning kit. "Rock fell in love with it because it was mathematical and precise," explains Tom. Rock began needlepointing Mark. "You should try it; it's a lot of fun." Rock began with pillows, then moved on to a big rug with American Indian patterns, which he transported with him on location in a special suitcase.

Every day at noon, Rock and Mark would go to the kitchen and eat lunch with Joy, the cleaning crew, and anyone else who happened to be there. Rock preferred a "casual house," where the staff was treated as family and they all ate together at the table with Rock. Mark referred to it as "the People's Republic of Hudson."

If it was late in the day and Rock and Mark were alone, they would clown. Mark would refer to Rock as "Trixie," a term George coined and that Rock loved since it had three meanings: he performed tricks, he was a benefactrix, and "tricks" was slang for sexual partners. Rock referred to Mark as a "treasured bird," a line from a W. C. Fields film.

"Treasured bird," said Rock, "it's time to practice our bows." Rock would give Mark his arm, Mark would accept it, and the two of them would strut about the home and grounds, mocking the way opera singers and huge stage players took their bows. They would sometimes start at the top of the grand staircase and come down smiling, arms extended and heads held high. They claimed to be in full costume, and the audience applauded. "It's not easy to go down the stairs," Mark admits. "You have to make a turn on the landing without ever looking down, and you have to maintain eye contact with the audience." They would bow as they got to the bottom of the stairs. The person playing the lady would curtsy, while the male would bow low. The object of the game was to see who would cry and laugh first. They'd both howl and tumble about on the carpet.

Tom Clark frequently came by on his way home from work for a drink. Tom had left M.G.M. to work for Rupert Allan, a private public-relations agency that represented Rock. Mark was working late one evening on correspondence. Tom came in for a drink and then went. Mark quickly departed, drove a few blocks, then remembered he'd left his wallet at home. He returned to grab it and noticed Tom Clark's car at the house. Mark exited the gate and drove home.

The friendship between Rock and Tom had grown steadily over the years. Tom was tall and commanding, with blue eyes and fair hair that was gradually turning white. He possessed a mellifluous voice that could carry through a stadium and spoke with an Oklahoma accent (he was raised in Oklahoma City, a Bible Belt Methodist). He was a vibrant presence, emotive and volatile, a wonderful storyteller and a skilled bridge player.

He and Rock first met in 1964, at Pat Fitzgerald's house, when Rock dropped by unexpectedly and took Tom's spot at the bridge table. Tom initially mistook Rock for "another self-involved actor," but they met at other parties and gatherings and learned they shared a sense of humor. They became close friends and lovers while both were still with other people over the years.

In 1972, Rock was invited to Australia to accept a "Logie," Australia's equivalent of an Emmy. He requested Tom to follow him as his publicist, and they took a break in Tahiti. Tom had never been to the South Pacific, and Rock had informed him that the sunsets were the best in the world. "We're going to see a sunset tonight," Rock stated. "We need martinis to toast this sunset." "I will go get them." There was no room service, so Rock went to get some drinks and returned with a plastic dishpan full of strange-looking liquid and bizarre little olives. "These are our martinis," remarked Rock. They showered, changed into white pants, went out to the deck, and lifted their martinis as the sun sunk into a cloud bank.

They tried again the next night. They were staying in the penthouse of a towering, new hotel on a different island. They requested martinis from room service, which arrived in perfect stem glasses. After showering, Rock said, "Let's just sit on the balcony in our towels and toast the sunset.""They settled in with their towels and martinis, and it was the most glorious sunset you had ever seen," Tom says. He walked into the room to get some refills, and on his way back, the door slammed shut behind him and latched. They had to descend a fire escape while holding scant towels over their privates and knock on windows until a cleaning lady opened a door. "That was Rock's ideal sunset." "But we had a great time in Australia," Tom says. "We discovered that we really worked well together." I coordinated everything and took care of what Rock required, as well as acting as a buffer. "Rock could never say no to anyone, whereas I could and did."

A television network in Buenos Aires invited Rock to film a show on his career the following year, 1973. Rock would not have gone if the show had not coincided with Mardi Gras, and Rock had long wanted to see Carnaval in Rio. McMillan and Wife had just been sold in South America, and Rock convinced Universal to send him on a three-week promotional tour. He requested Tom to follow him once more, and Tom had to take time off from his employment with Rupert Allan to do so.

Tom describes their journey as "another spectacular trip." Rock was nearly trampled by crowds in Buenos Aires, where Hollywood superstars are rarely seen. Rock and Tom ate world-famous Argentine steaks, flew in military helicopters around the countryside, and listened to gaucho music at a small club where they sat on couches and drank Scotch while the gauchos sang to them till early dawn.

They had a condominium overlooking Copacabana Beach in Rio de Janeiro. They attended formal balls and costume balls, where Rock was asked to judge, and were invited to sit in the governor's box for the Samba Parade, Mardi Gras' main event. Samba clubs, which are mainly created in underprivileged neighborhoods, practice their dances, gather funds, and prepare their costumes all year. Each club has a different theme and color scheme--one is all yellow, another all blue--and they pause to perform special songs when they dance past the governor's box. Rock and Tom stepped out into the street and started dancing with the clubs. "We got into samba lines, and people passed us bottles of beer, and we drank from them." The rain began to fall, but the samba groups continued to dance. Rock and Tom stayed in the box till daylight, sipping rum, eating and dancing in the streets.

It was one of those journeys that leaves individuals with a sense of adventure and recklessness, as well as a personal relationship to those who shared it with them. When it was time to leave Rio, Rock and Tom rushed to pack, collecting their clothing from the enormous closet in the suite, and Rock felt a wave of sadness: the vacation was coming to an end, and they would be returning to their separate lives. He grabbed some clothes and was stopped by Tom. "Those are really great items. "Don't mess with my fine things." Rock broke out laughing, amused by Tom's style of expressing himself. "Why don't you move in?" he replied, looking at him.

Tom called Mark and George when they returned to California. "May I come in?" Tom walked into their apartment "filled with fire and music, throwing handfuls of glitter dust," George remembers. Tom stated that he had never felt happier. "Rock has asked me to move in." George did not think it was a perfect match, but he and Mark agreed since "Rock is our friend." Mark and George fought with Tom when he said Rock wanted him to quit his job. "You've noticed folks coming and going in that residence. Rock wants them to all quit their jobs and remain at home, but the moment they do, Rock can't bear it."

"This is different," Tom commented. "He wants me to work for him and become an officer in the company."

Rock and Tom called Jack Coates to inform him of the situation. "What took you so long?" Jack asked. You have my approval."

At first, it appeared that Rock and Tom were a perfect match. They shared interests in bridge, dogs, drinking, football, traveling, casual dressing, reading, and listening to music. "Everything was spot on." "There wasn't a single discordant note," Tom explains. Tom had spent his whole adult life in the film industry, and he knew and respected everyone Rock knew. "I can take him anywhere," remarked Rock. "I can get him introduced to Princess Margaret." They traveled together and went out socially without hiding anything. They had a legitimate connection: Tom worked as a publicist for Rock and later as his personal manager.

Tom was nothing like the men Rock had previously dated. He wasn't a handsome young blond with a mustache. He was almost Rock's age, and he was a match. He confronted Rock and, more often than not, got his way. "I've always been looking for a Mark," Rock said of Mark and George, referring to someone who was loyal and supportive, who would do anything to assist his career, but who also had substance and intelligence. "I've never found it, and I hope I can with Tom."

Rock and Tom appeared to be content at the beginning. The first thing Rock asked when he got home from work was, "Where's Tom?"

"Upstairs," Mark explained.

"Thank you," Rock murmured before heading off to find him.

Around six o'clock, the two guys took a steam bath, then changed into floor-length robes, prepared beverages, and lit a fire in the outdoor fireplace. "How was your day?" They'd catch up, Tom would say. They might head into the playroom for a long record session if they weren't going out. "First, Rock got to pick something, and then I got to pick something," Tom explains. "We'd play big-band albums, Broadway musicals, and opera, and by the end, there'd be records all over the place, and poor Mark would have to come in the next day and sort them out." They drank all night and ate late, sometimes until midnight, so Joy would make dinner and leave it on the burner.

Everyone in the house began to drink more. Joy had become a heavy drinker, and Tom informed Rock, "We've got to get rid of that woman," but Rock refused. Because he had company, Rock drank more. Tom could drink as much as Rock, and on certain evenings, they both passed out. One of them would sneak into Mark's office in the morning and ask, "Could you go downstairs and find out from the staff what happened last night?" Because something happened that we don't understand. Check to see if there is anyone we should apologize to."

Tom was watching The $25, 000 Pyramid in the morning and couldn't be distracted between nine and nine-thirty. The staff dubbed him "Lana Lump-up, our lovely lady of Lullabye Lane," because he would say, "I'm gonna go upstairs and lump up," which meant he would curl up in his robe on the bed and watch television or read. When Tom moved in, Rock encouraged him, "Make the house yours," and he added, "I did, I absolutely did." He changed furniture, planted roses, and made sure the place was spotless. When he discovered how little the employees were being paid, he quickly gave them raises and made sure they received a substantial Christmas bonus--something Rock had not considered. "There was no doubt in the minds of anyone who came here: the house belonged to both of us," Tom adds.

Tom started using the word "we." "When we did McMillan..." he'd add, and he'd gush about "our dogs," "our car," and "our performance." He took over Rock's business and profession, as well as the house. He managed "our engagements," arranged reservations and appointments, and carried the cash.Rock lacked organization. He never made a plan. If things weren't going well at work, he couldn't fire somebody or make a scene. 'Who cares?' he'd ask. 'You're a movie star, goddammit!' I used to tell him. Will you act the part?'"

Tom studied scripts submitted to Rock, listened to proposals, and made recommendations on what Rock should do. "By what right does he do that?" many wondered. Mark Miller would simply shrug and add, "He just does."

Rock got resentful of Tom's desire for him to feel resentful of Tom. Tom was in charge of the gate. "Our worst fights were over that," Tom explains. "'Why do you do this?'" said Rock. 'Rock, because, A, you shouldn't, and B, you can't,' I said. I wanted to keep bad things from him. If there was a rumor, I attempted to keep it from him. If he found out anyway and discovered I knew, he was furious. He stated that I should have been the one to inform him."

After Tom came in, Rock's lifestyle began to change. Tom enjoyed "fine things" and the society of successful people. They bought a Rolls Royce, but Rock refused to drive it because he thought it was too flashy. "It didn't bother me at all," Tom jokes, "but I was born in that manner."

"Rock and I have decided to get rid of all the losers in Rock's life," Tom declared one day in Mark's office. We're going to clean them all up and start over." Friends who had been invited for ten years were abruptly removed from the guest list. "I can't get Rock on the phone, and Tom was very cold," they'd call Mark. "Why, what went wrong?" Mark would try to ease them down. "You've done nothing wrong. Give it some time."

The new group featured Ross Hunter and Jacque Mapes, Nancy Walker and her husband, David Craig, Roddy McDowall, Sylvia and Danny Kaye, and affluent socialite Olive Behrendt. Ross Hunter had produced eleven of Rock's films, but Rock had kept his distance since he didn't really trust him. "Come on, let's have him over, we'll have fun," Tom said, and he lined up a meal with Ross and Jacque. Rock began to appreciate Ross Hunter thanks to Tom's encouragement. He had a ruthless wit and could light up a room. The four became fast friends, regularly playing bridge, going on trips, and meeting for dinners.

They began holding intimate dinners for eight to twelve people, with everyone sitting at the same table and talking. On one night, they had Fred Astaire and Gene Kelly, and on another, they had Elizabeth Taylor and Carol Burnett. Pat and Michael York are a couple. Stephanie Powers and William Holden. Bette Davis was an actress. There were also larger "career parties." "Movie stars have to put on a good show," Tom remarks. When you'd rather have your excellent friends, you have to invite the president of NBC and M.G.M. to your house." Brunch was served on Sundays. Tom's task was to put the collar on the souffle dish and then prepare bull shots: vodka, beef bouillon, Tabasco, and lime, which Rock preferred to create with fresh Parmesan cheese. Lunches, bridge parties, and swimming parties were all held. When Rock and Tom weren't filming, they were out or entertaining seven nights a week.

Rock featured seventeen songs as well as a solo dance. Many performers in his position would have dismissed the challenge as reckless. "He had guts," Tony Randall adds. It takes guts to go out with a high-powered artist like Carol Burnett when you had no theatrical experience. Rock didn't waste time; he went to work."

Even more than television, the theater was a universe away from cinematic acting. In the theater, the performer must project to the last row of seats and enunciate well enough for every final t to be heard. Subtlety and underplaying, which were Rock's trademarks in films, don't work here. Rock had four weeks to prepare, and at that time, he shut out everything except the play. He worked with Jimmy Dobson in the mornings and Gower Champion in the afternoons. He instructed his workers that the front doorbell should not ring, the phones should not ring, and he should not be bothered. Rock would become enraged if someone made a noise on the terrace by accident. On June 13, 1973, the performance debuted in San Bernardino. Joy and Clarence, as well as Mark and George, Rupert Allan, and Jack Coates, drove out to see it. Everyone was tense. "I hope I'm not embarrassed for him," Jack said. "Oh shit, oh dear," Tom scrawled across the top of his appointment calendar in big letters. "We were scared to death," admits Tom. Backstage, he grabbed Rock and shouted, "You are going to kill them," then walked out into the audience, sat down, and "fell apart."

The event opened with Rock and Carol seated on opposite sides of the stage, preparing for their wedding. A draft in the theater had blown the curtain back across Rock's legs as he sat in a wing-back chair. When the music began, Rock felt the curtain being pushed up and away from him, "and there was this great black pit in front of me," he explained. "I almost died. My Adam's apple was pounding in my throat. Fortunately, when they saw us, the audience began to applaud. They applauded for so long that I had time to gather my wits and return my Adam's apple to its proper place." The first lyric of the show was written by Rock. He took a deep breath and started.

Rock was ecstatic at the after-show party. Mark approached him and remarked quietly, "Loved your bows." "It's all because of you," Rock said with a smile. "Inside this hulk is a frustrated song and dance man yelling to get out," Rock had often said, and it was true. On that first night, he fell in love with the theater. He liked getting an immediate reaction from the crowd; he liked knowing if the jokes made them laugh and if the show made them happy. He didn't have to wait ten months and check the box office to see how the movie was performing. In the theater, the personal interaction with the crowd was exciting.

Rock began chatting about Broadway in private. That was his next priority: get ready for Broadway. "He was like a dope addict," Tom explains. He was obsessed with the theater." Carol Burnett stated that she had never had so much fun on stage as she did with Rock. "Normally, I enjoy rehearsals and opening night, and after two more nights, I'm ready to call it quits." But we had so much fun with Rock that we decided to do it again. People would smash down doors simply to see Rock stand there and breathe, but he was absolutely amazing."

Rock and Tom planned a trip to Germany the next spring to buy a Porsche and drive through Italy and France so Rock could see Tom "Yourpe," as he called it. "When you go to another country, you should speak the language," Rock advised. "Let's take some French lessons." They went to Berlitz, but Tom left after only a few lessons.

"I'm no good at languages," he admitted to Rock, who persisted until the finish, which was an all-day, total immersion program in which he was only allowed to speak French. When he got home, his mind was racing. "Don't talk to me," he instructed Tom. "Make me a drink." "I'm unable to think."

This was the start of Rock and Tom's epic journeys. They took three or four journeys a year to every location on the planet that piqued their interest. Rock had always enjoyed traveling, and now he had a buddy who could accompany him whenever he wanted and would not raise suspicions. They took ocean liners and small private boat vacations, leased automobiles and planes, and traveled to Acapulco, Sicily, Baja California, Portugal and Spain, Yugoslavia and Italy, Australia, and Japan. They went to Mauna Kea on the island of Hawaii at least twice a year, which is one of the most gorgeous and opulent resorts in the world and Tom's favorite site to "lump up." The Greek Islands were the one place they wished to visit but never did. Rock told Tom shortly before his death, "I owe you that."

In the summer of 1974, Rock and Carol Burnett embarked on another I Do! I Do! tour. They had so much fun performing the play in Los Angeles that Carol's husband and producer, Joe Hamilton, booked halls in Dallas, Washington, D.C., and St. Louis. The performances were pre-sold out. They began in Dallas, where Rock and Tom rented a house and brought Joy, a friend of Joy's, to cook and keep her company. Rock refused to eat before the show, and it took him hours to recover afterwards. He and Tom would stand up and drink, then eat the dinner Joy had prepared and sleep until midday.

They performed at the Kennedy Center in Washington, D.C. A cousin of Tom's arranged for a tour of the White House, and Joy still has a photo of herself in the Rose Garden with Peggy, Rock, and Carol Burnett. They were booked into the Municipal Opera House in St. Louis, which was their first outdoor theater.

We climb into bed on stage the first night, right after we've been married. Carol is in her nightgown, and after some music, a gentle embrace, and a kiss, we go beneath the covers and the lights go out for the following scene. Except that the sun is still up in St. Louis at 8:30 a.m., and the stage is still well lit. So I glance at Carol beneath the covers and say, "Carol... we're going to have to have it, or... play tag." So, as Carol laughed, I slid out of bed and tiptoed behind it to prepare for the next performance.

71

The Scherer family had a significant contingent in St. Louis, and they organized a family reunion to coincide with Rock's concert at the Muni. "Rock was not enthusiastic," Tom explains, "because Scherer had deserted Rock and his mother." But Rock agreed to go, and his mother traveled out from California to see the play and attend the reunion with Mark Miller.

Despite the fact that it was June, Kay donned her mink coat and every piece of jewelry Rock had given her. "I'm so happy that we relinquished Roy to you," a woman relative told Kay at one point, "because you've done such a wonderful job raising him."

"What do you mean, relinquish?" Kay asked.

"Well, you know, you know, we could have kept him, but we felt he should be with you."

Kay reddened and remained silent. "Relinquish," she yelled as she rode back to the motel. Relinquish!" Rock and Tom laughed and encouraged her until she became enraged. Tom had another story to tell: he had been confronted by a Scherer relative who inquired, "Do you find me an honorable man?"

"Yes, sir, I most certainly do," Tom replied.

"I'm just a poor farmer." I've spent my entire life farming and trying to feed the hungry. "Do you think I'm worthy?"

"I do, indeed. Farmers are our country's backbone."

The cousin approached Tom. "Could you possibly get me on Let's Make a Deal?"

Mark Miller returned to California with Kay, and on the drive home from the airport, he had a chat with her that bothers him to this day. "Kay drove like a man," Mark observes. "She drove a T-Bird nicknamed 'the jukebox,' and her turn signal was always flickering." She used all four lanes of the freeway and would become enraged if motorists did not move over for her." "Did you notice that Roy doesn't look like any of the Scherers?" she whispered to Mark as she was driving and weaving. She looked ahead.

"Katherine," Mark asked, preparing himself for the next lane change, "do you mean what I think you do?"

"Mmmm," Kay remarked as she turned on the signal.

"She didn't confirm or deny," Mark explains, "and she wasn't the type of woman you could question." You'd be met with silence. Son is like his mum. It was interesting, though, that she brought it up. She didn't volunteer to have a chat."

Mark felt that Rock was not Scherer's son, that Kay was pregnant by another man, and that when Scherer discovered this, he abandoned the family. However, according to the birth certificate on file in Cook County, Illinois, Roy Harold Scherer is the father of Roy Harold Scherer, Jr., who was born on November 17, 1925. When Kay's relatives were informed of her chat with Mark, they stated that they had no idea what Mark suspected. "If it's true," one person added, "that's something Kay took with her to the grave."

Rock drafted a will in 1974 that directed that all of his assets be placed in a trust fund upon his death. All trust income would go to Tom Clark, and if Tom died, George Nader, and if George died, Mark Miller. Rock was aware that Mark and George pooled their monies, therefore it didn't matter which was mentioned first. When all three died, the trust's balance would be distributed to charities. Strangely, Rock determined that only one individual should benefit from the trust. Why didn't he split the food among the individuals he cared about? "It was like Rock to make it all or nothing," Mark explains. He didn't want people to become slackers and live off the money he'd worked so hard to obtain."

The following year, Rock hired Wallace Sheft as a new business manager. Rock was in debt despite earning a lot of money on McMillan and Wife for four years. Buddy Hackett had introduced Sheft to Rock, and he went out from New York to meet with Rock and Tom. Sheft is a tall man with thinning dark hair who doesn't mince words and peppers his discourse with Yiddish jargon. Rock expressed concern because Doris Day and other celebrities had been duped by those in charge of their finances. "I have a small C.P.A. firm in New York where I personally oversee and control everything," Sheft explained. My wife and I are uncomplicated people. I don't need and don't want your money."

He stated that his objective would be to make Rock financially independent, so that he could decide to produce a film not because he needed the money, but because he wanted to.

Rock and Tom exchanged glances and decided to entrust their finances to Wally Sheft right then and there. They then discovered that Sheft's childhood nickname was "tight wallets." He is obsessed with saving money and getting the greatest bargain possible. When Rock and Tom wanted to buy something, they had to clear it with Wally, who was only content if it was a good deal. He calculated that

Rock would require $250,000 each year to sustain his lifestyle, and that Sheft would eventually be able to make that amount through investments.

Joy, who had been with Rock for fourteen years, would have to leave as part of the housecleaning and renovating that followed Tom's arrival at Beverly Crest. "Joy would be having drinks with the company at dinner parties," Tom grumbled. He was also irritated that she was drinking on the job. "When we got home, there were unmade beds and cigarettes in the ashtrays, and Joy was drunk in her room." She should have been dismissed, but Rock didn't have the authority to do so."

Joy has been miserable since Tom moved in. He was dictatorial and condescending to her, and "when he was drinking," he was "downright nasty." The conflict grew unbearable. Joy was barely able to get from the stove to the table one night when Rock and Tom walked in for supper. She wobbled over with a saucepan in her hand, supported herself on a chair, and began serving little peas and mashed potatoes. She reached into the pot for the peas, but she didn't notice Rock's plate and spooned them onto the table. "Watching Joy unable to hit the plate," Tom couldn't help but chuckle, but Rock grabbed her up, carried her down the hall to her room, and flung her on the bed. "I don't want to see you again until you've been sober for two days," he said emphatically.

Joy couldn't remember what had happened the night before. "Did I do something wrong last night?" she wondered aloud to Tom.

"Did you ever?"

Rock was done with Joy after that, and once he was done with someone, it was over. His own drinking, he felt, had never interfered with his work, but Joy's drinking had.

Soon after, Tom and Joy got into an argument in which Tom shouted at her and she hurled a box of cottage cheese across the room. "You've got to deal with Joy," Tom stated to Rock. "I can't take it any longer."

Rock informed Joy that he desired an all-male residence. He was getting older and desired the freedom to do as he pleased in his home, including walking naked if he so desired. "When I walk through those doors, I want to be alone." Joy requested that the handyman assist her in loading her belongings into his pickup truck and driving her to her son's place.

Following Joy's departure, there was a flurry of persons passing through the Castle, including housemen and butlers who were unpleasant and did not survive long, until James Wright was hired in 1978.

In 1975, Rock turned fifty, and Tom celebrated with a costume birthday party that he subsequently described as "the prettiest party we ever had." He took everything out of the house and put it in the playroom. He transformed the crimson room into a nightclub, complete with a dance floor, a band, a bar, and small tables. The spacious living room was transformed into a dining room, with eight tables draped with brown tablecloths, silver candelabra, and chocolate-brown candles.

Dozens of potted ficus trees were brought in and illuminated with small bulbs. There were so many flowers that the air was fragrant, and an electric train was whirling round and round at Rock's table because Rock had never had one.

Several hours before the celebration, Rock and Tom got into a yelling match. As the arrival time drew, Tom became more concerned, and Rock attempted to undercut his preparations.

"We can't use the playroom--why did you put everything in there?" Rock said.

"What do you expect me to do with it?" "Be quiet."

"Fucked you."

"Flick you."

Tom slammed the door, left the house, and went to a T-shirt shop to have a shirt made that proclaimed, in large letters, ROCK IS A PRICK. He handed the garment to Rock as a birthday gift.

As the visitors arrived, Rock remained upstairs. Arab costumes were the most popular that year, and Buddy Hackett, Rupert Allan, and Mark Miller dressed up as Arabs. Tom was dressed in kilts. Carol Burnett and Joe Hamilton dressed up as flappers because Rock was born in the 1920s. Fans such as Olive Behrendt, Roddy McDowall, Nancy Walker, and David Craig arrived and stood outside the door, screaming and requesting autographs. Juliet Mills and Michael Miklenda rode their motorcycles right through the front door and onto the patio.

"It was one of those parties that actually worked," Tom explains. The fires were blazing, the small lights were twinkling, music was playing, and beverages and food were flowing. Rock and Tom continued to move around. "We both worked our tails off," adds Tom. "You've gotta work the room." They had a drink in the bar in the middle of the evening.

"Thanks, babe," Rock replied. "It's a great party."

Rock was in his prime. He had lived for half a century and was a star among stars on this night. Heaven and earth were in their rightful places.

Chapter 8

Rock traveled to London in December 1975 to appear in I Do! I Do! alongside Juliet Prowse. The producers had approached Tom and urged him to assist them in starting a subscription theater. "OK," Tom said. We want a riverfront room at the Savoy, a car and driver, and £500 per week." "Who the hell will we get as our leading lady?" he wondered. Carol Burnett was unavailable, Lee Remick, who resided in London, declined, and then Juliet Prowse's representative called to say she was interested. Rock and Tom were invited to see Juliet's act at the Desert Inn in Las Vegas.

When Rock and Tom arrived and spotted Juliet's name on the marquee, Rock exclaimed, "Do you realize, we've come to audition a headliner?" Rock and Tom went to her dressing room after the show, and Rock told her, "I think you're wonderful." Would you mind doing what I Do! I Do! with me?"

Juliet had dinner with Rock and Tom every night after the play in a restaurant that stayed open for them. "There was a lot of tension between Rock and Tom," Juliet remembers, "and it was fueled by all the drinking." 'Another tiny triple?' Tom would ask, and out would come another round of triple gin martinis with an orange twist."

When Rock and Tom returned from London, Mark and George sensed a shift in their relationship. What had begun as friendly sparring-"You're wrong." "No, no, I'm not." "Yes, you are!" -was becoming grating. Rock and Tom were constantly arguing, each attempting to prove the other wrong."Rock loved a good fight, and Tom was a fighter," George explains, but Rock was developing a cruel side, and Tom had two personas. "He was a fantastic monster." He was compassionate, loyal, generous, and wonderfully charming when he was sober. He was nasty and insulting when he was intoxicated. He'd sever your heart and never look back." His divided personality made him unpredictable. "We learned through the years not to cross him," Mark adds. "You had problems the moment you crossed him, because Rock would turn around and side with the monster."

Rock and Tom never clashed over major matters. "Something major would happen, and they'd band together," Mark predicts. What they fought over was insignificant. When Tom was employed, he went out and bought outfits for James Wright, but Rock warned him not to wear them.

"Get your ass in that uniform," Tom advised.

"Take it off," Rock instructed. "Don't pay any attention to Tom."

"Don't pay any attention to Rock."

Mark Miller was frequently caught in the crossfire. "We're not going on the Q. E.II.," Rock would say into his office. "Please cancel the reservation." Later, Tom would walk in and say, "Book the reservation." Don't tell Rock anything. And don't tell Wally Sheft that it will cost $13,000 to travel to England. I've never been on a ship before, and I'd like to go."Alcohol intensified their argument. When Rock drank, he became "a viper," according to Mark, and used Tom as his whipping boy. When Tom entered the room, Rock would taunt him. "Oh, Tommy Truth." "What lies have you got for us today?"

"Fuck you," Tom would say as he exited the room. "I hope he dies a terrible death, bald," Tom would say in front of his buddies. I really hope he doesn't wake up. We'll all be better off, and God willing, I'll be wealthy. "I have the freedom to do whatever I want."

Most of their friends learnt to ignore the squabbling and had no doubts that beneath it all was a strong friendship. "People can spend their lives bickering and really love each other," explains Jon Epstein, a longtime friend who produced McMillan and Wife. I assumed it would go on indefinitely." "Tom loved and protected Rock magnificently, but Rock didn't want so much protection," explains Stockton Briggle, who directed Rock in Camelot. Tom had sacrificed a brilliant career to become 'Mrs. Rock Hudson.' It's difficult to respect someone who abandons his own life and begins doing everything for you. They were never able to deal with it. They simply drank more, socialized more, and traveled more."

In the summer of 1976, during America's bicentennial year, Rock toured in Stephen Vincent Benet's production of John Brown's Body. It was a narrative poem that had previously been performed by Tyrone Power and Dame Judith Anderson. Rock had seen Power's performance with Bob Preble and had fallen in love with him. "All he could talk about was Tyrone Power," adds Preble. When Rock met Power, they flirted about becoming together but never did.

Rock was overjoyed when Tom asked him to do John Brown's Body: "I've never had such beautiful words to say." They secured Claire

Trevor and Leif Erickson as co-stars and started off in great spirits. However, due to bad administration, the tour had to be canceled. They were booked on college campuses, but most were unoccupied during the summer, so they played to empty households. However, Rock garnered the best reviews of his career. Flo Allen contacted Rock and read him the Variety review, which said, "Hudson proves himself a fine actor, revealing a strong side to his dramatic talent that has seldom been explored by films... Hudson should now be able to take his place in the ranks of exceptional stage performers."

When he heard it, Rock burst into tears, and Jon Epstein had the evaluation framed. "After decades of bad reviews," Tom recalls, "I can't tell you what this meant."

The production had a chorus of young performers who traveled by bus, while Rock, Claire, and Tom took limos and Leif flew his own jet. Tom gathered the group in the hotel lounge, where there was a piano bar, on their first night off in Spokane, Washington. "I made it my job to be the social director," adds Tom. "The star has to keep the company happy, make everyone feel like a family, and keep things fun, or it shows in the production." "OK, you kids, we don't know who you are," Tom stated to the young performers. "Stand up and sing!" They sang in turns, then said to Rock and Claire, "We don't know you, get up and sing." Rock sang "Send in the Clowns," Claire performed "Moanin' Low," and Tom performed "You Are My Sunshine." "We all fell in love, it was one of the most magical nights of all time," Tom adds. The hotel guests began applauding and leaning over the balcony. We then stated, "Get rid of the limo, we're taking the bus with the kids."

When the performance was in San Francisco, Rock and Tom dined with a group of guys that included Armistead Maupin, whom Jack Coates had introduced to Rock. Armistead is a writer and a well-known LGBT character in San Francisco, with his multivolume novel Tales of the City serialized in the San Francisco Chronicle. Armistead looked up to Rock Hudson as a role model. "Rock was manly, successful, kind hearted, funny, and gay," Armistead says. "He'd overcome the obstacles that a gay person faces and made it big."

The night Armistead had supper with Rock happened to be the night before his debut column appeared in the Chronicle. After dinner, they returned to Rock's Fairmont hotel, where Rock secretly went to the desk and grabbed a copy of the next day's paper. After everyone had been seated and given drinks, Rock stood up and read the first installment of Tales of the City. Armistead was "blown away," witnessing his words brought to life and magnified with meaning by Rock Hudson. There were glimmers of affection and admiration between them, and it seemed like the start of a friendship.

The next night, Armistead met Rock and Tom for supper at La Bourgogne, their favorite restaurant in town. Armistead informed Rock that he had only recently come out publicly and with his family. "I've been enjoying my life more and finally feeling in control of it." "It could make a big difference to a lot of people," he said, if Rock disclosed the truth about his life, possibly in a book. It would have a huge impact on eradicating some of the preconceptions about gays. It would be incredible if you revealed the entire thing."

Tom Clark said, "Not until my mother dies."

They laughed and went on, and Armistead could tell Rock was intrigued but "wasn't ready."

Rock toured in Camelot the following year, 1977, and it was, in Tom's words, "the best summer that ever was." Rock's favorite role was King Arthur. It was a flamboyant role, with difficult acting opportunities and fantastic melodies, and Rock identified with Arthur. The piece was autumnal, about past glories, and it resonated with Rock's autumnal attitude.

Tom and Rock headed to New York to select a director and cast members. Bill Ross, the producer, had a tight relationship with Stockton Briggle, who had previously directed musicals for him. Stockton is an eloquent man from Texas with sandy hair, fair skin, and wire-frame glasses. He has a flair for spotting the humor in situations and a contagious enthusiasm for his work. He was a fan of Rock's and wanted to direct Camelot, but Ross replied, "I don't think you've got much of a chance." They've been seeing a lot of big filmmakers."

Stockton came to California to work with Rock three months before rehearsals began. They sat in their bathing suits by the pool, poring over the book, trying to figure out why the story had never worked.

Rock's mother died after a stroke in the fall of 1977. Rock had taken her on a bridge cruise around the world the previous year. She'd gotten the flu twice and never really recovered. Rock declined to go see her after she became bedridden. "I can't handle it," he said to

Mark. "Will you go down there?" Rock did not visit his mother for the last six months of her life, and he later expressed regret. "Because I remember her as she was-a real goin' Jessie, driving, speeding, a whirlwind."

Mark would go down to Newport Beach every two weeks to check on Kay, go grocery shopping, and make sure the housekeeper was present and had enough money. The housekeeper was a Central American woman named Bezelia, who was a relative of Claire Trevor's housekeeper. Kay was nice and polite to Bezelia, but when she saw Mark, she said, "Why won't my son come?"

"Darling, he's very busy." "He's swamped with work and can't get away," Mark explained.

Claire Trevor contacted Rock late one night in October and said, "Your mother's had a stroke." Even though Rock and Tom were inebriated, they hopped in their car and drove down to Newport Beach. Kay had died by the time they arrived. Rock walked into the bedroom by himself for a while before exiting. He didn't cry, but he was heartbroken. His mother was the only blood family with whom he felt bonded. When he was younger, it was just the two of them against the world, but he never mentioned it. "It was much too private," Tom observes. "He would never expose those emotions to anyone." Mark would occasionally catch Rock staring into space, but it was the only visible indicator that he was in mourning.

Rock had just begun filming Wheels, a mini-series, and the producer offered to adjust the schedule so that Rock could take a few days off, but Rock declined. He needed to work and headed to the studio the following morning.

Mark and George made funeral arrangements, but Rock refused to go. They were stunned, but they cooperated. When December arrived, Rock stated that he could not spend Christmas at home since it would be too difficult without his mother. "Let's get outta town," he remarked to Tom, and they boarded a train bound for New Mexico. Rock abandoned all of his customs, refusing to buy a tree or exchange gifts.

Rock had begun what Mark would refer to as "the decline." He was drinking so much gin that the booze was seeping through his pores, and "his breath was awful." He grew swollen. Mark was unable to conduct any business with Rock or Tom until noon. "In the morning and at two p.m., I'd make plans with them." I'd discover they hadn't understood a word I'd spoken. Every night, they'd stay up late and fall asleep inebriated. Rock would wake up at two o'clock in the afternoon and begin needlework in my office, while Tom would watch old movies." When Rock was shooting, he'd drink all night but have to get up at 7 a.m. for a call. "Get me a drink," he said as soon as he got home. "

George became irritated and enraged as he watched Rock damage himself. "He was given so much; he could portray greatness." Only a few people on the planet are given the gift of portraying what is good and honorable, and he was wasting it."

Rock's disposition, which had always been sunny, was darkening. His favorite phrase was, "Fuck him, I hope he dies." After a dinner party hosted by a friend, Rock exclaimed, "Fuck him, I hope he dies." He envied everyone else's prosperity or good fortune. If he learned that another celebrity owned a 65-foot yacht, he'd wonder, "Where does he get the money for a yacht?" "I'm hoping it sinks." He was irritated when he watched Richard Gere in Bent in New York. "What's the big deal?" Gere was not my favorite actor."

Some of Rock's pals believed he wouldn't be able to handle becoming an older guy. He'd be a grandfather in ten years. "This is a cruel business," explains Stockton Briggle. "You're given the world, and what do you do when it's taken away?" Rock had had his pick of the most gorgeous men in the country for twenty years, and now there was a tinge of patronization when young guys spoke to him.

He refused to serve dinner until ten o'clock. When everyone was seated, Rock would recount anecdotes, and just as he got to the punch line, Tom would stop, saying, "No, no, you're telling it wrong."

"Not at all. I'm familiar with the story.

"You're telling it wrong!"

"All right, you tell me the fucking story."

Tom would go upstairs and pass out at some point throughout the evening, but Rock would stay until the finish, no matter how intoxicated he was, scared he would miss something.

Rock and Tom recruited butler James Wright shortly before Christmas in 1978. James arrived at the interview with reservations. "I didn't want to work for a movie star because they're volatile," James explains. He had previously worked for Universal's president, William Goetz, and A. H. Meadows, a Dallas oilman. "I had to be smartly dressed all the time in a black suit and tie," he adds of both positions, "and I would say, 'Madam' and 'Sir.'" James was born in England, nurtured in an orphanage, and taught to be the type of butler seen in old movies, who enters into the exquisite drawing room carrying a silver tray with glasses of sherry and announces, "Madam dinner will be served in fifteen minutes."

Tom started the interview with James, then Rock took over, showed him around the house, and said, "When can you move in?" James moved in with his small puppy, Victoria, on Christmas Eve, expecting to be gone in two weeks. "It wasn't me," he clarifies. "I'm used to a house that's debonair and sophisticated, with beautifully laid tables." Mr. Hudson preferred people to be relaxed, and he occasionally ate standing up at the refrigerator. I could wear whatever I wanted, including shorts and T-shirts. And I had two bosses, which was challenging. Mr. Hudson was the key guy for me, and he was simple to get along with. Mr. Clark was fluffy and zealous. Everything had to be perfect. 'Dust dust dust!' he'd say. 'What's the deal with the dust up there?' "We had a wind today, that's why," I'd explain. This morning, it was cleaned."

Rock welcomed James into "the family" almost immediately. Because the kitchen is the heart of the house, and James was constantly there, standing behind the counter, invincible, James soon understood everything that was going on. He demonstrated that he could be trusted not to speak to the press and that he was a man of his word.

As Rock's interest in theater expanded, he and Tom found themselves spending more time in New York. In May 1979, Rock purchased an apartment in Beresford on Central Park West and 81st Street that Tom had found. Rock enjoyed wandering around the city and riding the subways; he liked the small-town feel of the area, where he could stroll to the market and the drugstore and knew everyone by name. He and Tom went to plays, met people in the theater, and made new acquaintances. "We'd gotten stuck in a rut in L.A., and we loved the change of scenery," Tom explains. "We were very social." We didn't spend a single night at home."

They left in June for a five-month tour of On the Twentieth Century, a play Rock insisted on doing but became tired of as the run progressed. Dean Dittman, one of his co-stars, would become a close friend for the rest of his life. Dean is a big man who used to weigh

300 pounds and is a talented character actor who played Daddy Warbucks in Annie. He loves to cook and entertain, and after the show ended, he invited Rock and Tom to many dinners at his place. Rock realized that the show was in financial difficulties in Chicago and took a pay reduction to keep the production solvent until they reached Los Angeles, where they had a subscription audience. Rock agreed to meet Tom for supper at Joe Allen's after the play one night in Los Angeles. "Rock was able to drive from the theater to the restaurant only because I had dropped bread crumbs," Tom explains. They had dinner before heading to Dean Dittman's for a cast party. They drank a lot at Dean's and then drove home in two automobiles. Tom drove the Mercedes, believing Rock was immediately behind him in the Seville, and arrived home first, collapsing on the bed.

Rock nodded out behind the wheel and slammed into a palm tree on Doheny Road, totaling the Cadillac. He crawled out the door and began strolling up the street, glass fragments buried in his brow. A milkman noticed him and contacted the cops.

"I'm okay," Rock said.

"Who was driving?" inquired the officer.

"Tom Clark."

The cops brought Rock home and returned to the bushes in search of Tom Clark, who was sleeping upstairs. James attempted to wake Tom but was unsuccessful, so he summoned Mark and George. "Come over right now, there's been an accident!" When Mark and George took Rock to the hospital to have the glass removed, George was amazed that Rock had not been gravely injured. "Another example of an angel on his shoulder."

Sex had taken second place in the early years, when Rock was single-mindedly pursuing his job, but as his career faded, sex became dominant. Rock thrived on mystery and conquest. "The chase was over the minute the prey fell into the lair, and a new one began," a buddy adds. Rock was attracted to a variety of collaborators, including airplane stewards in San Diego and carpenters and maitre d's in New York. He threw all-male events, such as the beauty party, where he didn't know the majority of the attendees.Rock spent the weekend in San Francisco with Tom, Mark, and George in July 1978. They dined with Jim Gagner and Armistead Maupin at the "Duck House" on Telegraph Hill, which had a frieze of geese flying over the top of the building. After dinner, Armistead took everyone to Club Fugazi to see Beach Blanket Babylon, a revue he co-wrote. Then Mark and George went back to the Fairmont to sleep, while Rock and Tom went on a homosexual club tour with Armistead.

The next morning, during breakfast at the Fairmont, Rock delivered a thorough account that shocked and scared George, prompting him to write in his journal, "My GOD." George said Rock enjoyed "shocking the hell out of me, like I was a fuddy-duddy, the straitlaced country cousin." George had always avoided gay meetings, and the description of clubs where mass intercourse occurred between strangers seemed to him to be the beginning of the end of civilization. This was a moment when gay sex had achieved a pinnacle of tolerance and permissiveness, and the terrible irony is that this was also the time when the AIDS epidemic was taking hold. Rock had gone to these clubs where he could be recognized and had even signed his name, which irritated George. "I wanted to see it," Rock explained, "because you should see everything in life." Rock, on the other hand, stated that he was taken aback by how promiscuous things had become.

The next stop was the Black and Blue club. "This is too much for me," Tom Clark exclaimed after one peek inside. I'm returning to the motel. "You guys keep going." A motorcycle hung from the ceiling, while men dressed in boots and black leather jackets stood around the bar. At midnight every night, they played "Thus Spake Zarathustra," the 2001 theme song. Pieces of corrugated metal were hanging from the ceiling in the back of the club, forming three orgie zones. It was like something out of a Bosch film: a heap of naked arms, legs, backs, and wiggling behinds. Armistead and Rock were standing against the wall, observing, and Rock found it amusing. "How ironic," Armistead recalls thinking. I'm standing next to the man who was the world's sex symbol for two decades, and no one is paying attention to him. We could go through here like two women-- completely undetected." Armistead leaned over and jokingly pinched Rock.

"Is that you?" Rock said.

"Yes."

"Just double-checking."

After men began dying of AIDS, the Glory Holes, like other gay clubs and bathhouses, closed down a few years later. "It may sound like the end of civilization," Armistead adds, "but there were good people there, people with intelligence and humor." There was a sense of trust and community that was extremely healthy." He claimed that the clubs arose at a period when a huge number of guys were coming out and needed to be accepted by a large number of other men. "The place was a real escape," he recalls. "No matter what your worries of the day had been, you could find complete abandonment there."

Chapter 9

Rock agreed to make another NBC series, The Devlin Connection, about a father and son police duo, in 1981. After McMillan and Wife, Rock vowed never to do another TV series. "As you get older, you learn to keep your mouth shut more," he told a reporter, "because you never know how badly you're going to embarrass yourself later."

NBC wanted Rock back on the air and had done everything they could to convince him. Rock explained to his friends, "I like to work." For his son's co-star, he cast a young and inexperienced actor, Jack Scalia, who had previously worked with him in the miniseries The Star Maker. Rock had grown fond of Jack and had gotten to know him and his wife. Rock contacted Jack twenty minutes after he was told he received the part and stated, "It's important for us to start a father-son relationship, so it will carry over onto the screen." Jack lived a few blocks away from Rock on Central Park West, so they started walking about New York.

Jack kissed Rock on the cheek and held him from the start, "because that's the relationship I had with my own father." I could see Rock was uncomfortable at first, but he got used to it." As they walked, Rock would bombard Jack with questions. Jack had been hooked on drugs and alcohol and had "gone sober" in 1979, and Rock was curious about the experience. But when Jack questioned Rock, he never received an explanation.

"There were a lot of parallels between Rock and me and the characters we were playing," Jack explains. Rock was Brian Devlin, and Jack was his son, Nick Corsello, whom Rock had abandoned and hadn't seen since he was a newborn. The characters didn't know one other and were getting to know one another. "Nick had a lot of knowledge about his father, but he didn't know him," Jack adds. "I knew a lot about Rock, but I didn't know him." And Nick had a deep affection for his father."

"What does it feel like to have a son?" Jack asked Rock one afternoon as they walked by the Museum of Natural History.

"I'm not sure. I'll let you know as soon as I get one."

"Cut that shit out," Jack instructed. "My name is Nick Corsello. "It's your son."

"Oh. That's the one." Rock burst out laughing.

"How come you never talk to me directly?"

"Who, me?"

"How come you don't answer me directly?"

"What exactly do you mean by that, Jack?"

"Don't get started on that, Rock."

"I'm not going to begin. "I'm curious what you mean by that."

"When I ask you a direct question, you don't give me an immediate answer."

"There are many ways to answer a question," Rock explained.

"Why don't you give me the one I really want?"

"Maybe because you want it, Jack."

Jack would give up in despair. "It was almost like a sword fight." Parry and thrust, parry and thrust, parry and thrust. That was his method of preventing you from learning too much about him."

Rock, on the other hand, demonstrated to Jack how much he cared for him. Except for Rock and Tom, Jack knew no one when he moved to California for the show. "I had two adoring fathers. They advised me on where to reside and assisted me in finding a place." Rock referred Jack to his dentist, Dr. Phillip Tennis, because he needed work done on his teeth. Rock called the day of his appointment to say he was going to take Jack to the dentist for the first time. "You might feel a little more at ease." After Rock presented him to the dentist, Jack entered the examination room, sat on the chair, and heard a knock on the door. "Who is it?" remarked Dr. Tennis, winking at Jack.

Rock pushed open the door and peered inside. "Would you like me to come in?"

"No, but please come sit down," Jack said. "I know you'll be happier." Rock then proceeded to crack jokes and keep Jack smiling for an hour while the dentist operated on him, according to Jack. "Rock Hudson came to my house today, drove me to my dentist, told me jokes for an hour while I sat in the chair, then drove me home," Jack told a friend that evening. "Are you telling me that this isn't a make-believe world in Hollywood?"

Jack realized he and Rock had similar temperaments. They were both Scorpios born in November, and they were both secretive and private. "We're a lot alike, but we're also different," Rock added. "You think so?" You're not as obstinate as I am. Jack stated.

"Yes, and I'm going to show you."

They started playing a game in which Rock would stop at the door and insist on Jack going first whenever they went out together. They once stood for fifteen minutes outside Jimmy's restaurant in Beverly Hills.

"The last time," Jack continued, "I went in first." "You get to go first this time."

Rock folded his arms and shook his head.

"I'm not going to go first again," Jack declared.

"All right, we'll eat our lunch here." We'll have them bring dinner out. Waiter!"

"Okay, I'll go in!" Jack stated.

"I told you I was ten times more stubborn than you."

Rock and Jack were heading out of their trailers on the first day when they noticed buzzards circling in the sky. They were informed that a man had asphyxiated himself in a nearby car. Rock examined the automobile, the buzzards, and then Jack. "And it's only our first day of work," he pointed out.

Rock did not directly assist Jack, but he did make himself accessible to rehearse and make comments. If Jack appeared to be struggling with a scene, Rock would approach him and ask, "You feel okay? Do you want to run the lines? Let's chat about it for a few minutes."

"This is my first big job, I'm working with Rock Hudson, and I was frenetic," Jack says. I'd like to run the lines 400 times in five minutes, and he'd sit there with me." "Why are you doing all of this?" Jack inquired of Rock.

Jane Wyman went out of her way to support Rock when he was new to acting and making Magnificent Obsession. When he questioned why, Jane replied, "If we have anything to give another person, it's the experience we've had." So I'm handing it to you, and I know you'll pass it on someday." "It's my turn to pass it on now," Rock stated to Jack. Jack sobbed as he walked back to his trailer.

Jack began referring to Rock as "the big guy," and the writers incorporated it in the scripts. Rock, according to Jack, was not six feet four, as he has always claimed, but six six. "I'm six one, and Rock towered over me." I've played a lot of basketball and stood next to a lot of big players, but Rock wasn't six four. He had huge hands that could encompass my entire face." They had one sequence in which Rock was meant to slap Jack after he insulted him. "Coming from the New York School of Acting, I said, 'Rock, you better hit me, so I can get the full effect.'"

"You sure?" Rock asked.

"I believe it would work in this scene." Give me a good smack."

Jack claims he never saw Rock's hand, but only felt it. "It's called 'ringing your bell,' and it's similar to the sixty-second warning before a nuclear attack." Jack flubbed a sentence after being hit, and the scene had to be reshot. He was standing there, clutching his jaw, when Rock asked, "Well?"

"Rock, you had better hit me again."

Rock gave him another bell-ringing smack, and Jack spoke everything correctly. "That was very good," commented Rock as he approached.

"It was good because I didn't want to get hit a third time."

"I was wondering when you'd come to your senses," Rock remarked.

They had finished three episodes and were halfway through the fourth when Rock awoke in the middle of the night with shooting pains in his chest. When Tom returned downstairs at 6 a.m., Rock was white and his arm was numb all the way to his fingertips. "I'm glad you're up," he commented. "I can hardly breathe." Tom raced him to Cedars-Sinai Hospital's emergency room, where they performed a cardiogram and discovered no evidence of a heart attack. He returned to work, but his doctor, Rex Kennamer, ordered a battery of tests.

Rock had experienced shortness of breath and chest pains while going home from a restaurant in New York, but he dismissed it as indigestion. He was pleased with his physical condition and stamina. If he caught a cold on Monday, he'd be fine by Tuesday, while the rest of the family would sniffle and suffer all week. "I'm going to live to be a hundred, and the rest of you will be dead," Rock regularly stated.

Dr. Kennamer discovered indications of blockages in three coronary arteries when the test results were returned, and he advised Rock to enter the hospital for emergency bypass surgery. The Devlin Connection's production was halted, and Rock was anxious about Jack. "No matter what happens," he told the studio executive in charge, "I want you to take care of the kid."

The night before his surgery, Rock gazed out his hospital room window at the word HOLLYWOOD engraved in the mountainside. "I wonder if I'll ever see that sign again," he reflected.

"Oh, come on," Tom exclaimed. "You have the best doctors in the world, and you are strong."

"I can't help but think that if I leave now, I'll have a fantastic time." He chatted with Mark Miller and Dean Dittman on the phone. "I'm bidding farewell to Hollywood and all my friends in the hills," he remarked. Rock later told Mark that he believed they had spoken for the last time.

Rock survived the surgery, which evolved into a quintuple bypass, and recovered with amazing speed. Tom donated blood to replace the blood Rock had received, and it occurred to Tom in 1985 that Rock may have caught AIDS as a result of blood transfusions. Cedars-Sinai was located in West Hollywood, which had a sizable LGBT community. At the time of Rock's bypass surgery in 1981, no one in his circle of acquaintances had heard of AIDS. They were hearing tales in the LGBT world about a rare cancer that was killing homosexuals-"There's something out there, be careful"-but it had no name.

Dr. Michael Gottlieb of UCLA and Dr. Alvin Friedman-Kien of NYU alerted the Centers for Disease Control in Atlanta in 1981 that they had identified several cases of two rare diseases in gay men-Pneumocystis carinii pneumonia and Kaposi's sarcoma-both of which are typically seen in people with a weakened immune system. AIDS was identified as a novel and different disease as a result of reports from other doctors in major cities. In 1982, the first pieces on it appeared in prominent magazines. AIDS was thought to be spread sexually, but there was no link to blood transfusions at the time.

When Rock was diagnosed with AIDS in 1984, Dr. Gottlieb said it was "virtually impossible to determine with certainty" where Rock got the disease. This was true for all sexually transmitted diseases, he continued, "because the true number of lovers is known only to the person who has the disease."

Three days after the bypass surgery, Jack Scalia went to see Rock. He was still in pain, and Jack supported him in bed. Rock expressed his desire to return home and light a cigarette.

"Are you out of your mind?" Jack stated.

"This is a test." I'm only going to smoke one."

"That's a lot of shit."

"I can do anything I want," Rock declared.

"I know you can," I say, "but if you smoke one, you'll start smoking again."

On the bed, Jack's hand was not far from Rock's. Rock reached over and placed his hand on Jack's--his first foray into physical contact. A tear trickled down his cheek as his eyes welled up.

"What's going on?" Jack stated.

"I'm terrified. "I'm terrified."

More tears flowed.

"It's all right," Jack softly murmured, "it's all right to do this."

When Rock lifted his head after a minute, his eyes were dry. "No. I'm ok. I'll be just fine."

"You're a son of a bitch, Rock, for stopping." What you were doing was incredibly special. "I wish you had continued."

"I'm not going to. "I'm all right."

Rock's ability to turn it off so quickly astounded and scared Jack. "I sensed a strong sense of loneliness in him. He'd gotten too good at protecting himself; he never shared his life with anyone."

The following week, Tom brought Rock home from the hospital and discovered him smoking in the kitchen a few days later. "I got up in the middle of the night, came downstairs, and lit a cigarette, and I don't care," Rock admitted. "I knew there was no point in arguing," Tom recalls. He smoked right up until the end, and cigarettes didn't kill him, did they?"

To quit smoking, Rock and Tom tried a variety of methods. They'd heard of the "hip hypnotist," Pat Collins, who performed at nightclubs. "We need to stop smoking," Tom remarked when he called her. Do you want to come over and have some cocktails?" Pat arrived in formal attire, complete with heavy makeup and jewelry. She and her secretary were conversing and drinking in the living room when Rock started, "Well, we want to stop smoking." She led Rock and Tom up to the bedroom, had them lie down on the sofa with their eyes closed, talked to them, and planted the suggestion. When she went, neither Rock nor Tom knew if they had survived. "We lit up so fast your head would spin," recounts Tom.

Rock's diet did not change following the procedure. He continued to eat gizzards, which are high in cholesterol, and he ate them with a lot of salt and butter. He did not participate in cardiac rehabilitation activities, although he did begin walking. "Let's walk around the Hollywood reservoir," Jack Scalia would offer. "I'll come get you." Rock was able to reduce his drinking from fifteen to two drinks per day. Rock, according to Mark Miller, would occasionally get drunk one night and then not get drunk again for three weeks. "He woke up from the drunkenness of the seventies," George explains. "The sniping and meanness faded, and he was returning to the Rock we knew in 1952--a warm human being who laughed and played games." Rock felt as if he'd been granted a reprieve; he assessed his life and resolved to rectify everything that had made him unhappy.

His physicians told him that if he survived the first year, he had a fair chance of living a normal life. He was warned that he would experience moments of forgetfulness, anger, or paranoia, particularly a fear of traveling, but that he might look forward to enhanced sexual vitality.

Although not anticipated, the show's failure was a setback for Jack Scalia, who did not see Rock as frequently after they parted ways. Rock dropped by Jack's house for a tree-trimming party during Christmas, and while conversing with Jack and the actress Stepfanie Kramer, who appeared in Hunter, Rock remembered a Christmas he experienced as a child in Winnetka. Rock recalled his stepfather, Wally Fitzgerald, buying him a Flexible Flyer for Christmas when he was eight years old. Rock had been wanting the sled for a year and went out to ride it with his pal Billy immediately away. On the first day, he had an accident and wrecked the sled, which he hid at Billy's. Wally kept inquiring where the sled was and eventually walked over to Billy's where he found it split in half in the garage. Rock claimed his stepfather slapped him and swore he'd never give him another sled again.

When Rock was brought home from his ill-fated vacation to Paris and was at UCLA Medical Center in the summer of 1985, Jack requested Stepfanie to help him think of a gift to bring Rock to the hospital. "It's a big deal, he's coming home, and I want to get him something."

"I know exactly what he'd like," Stepfanie added. She enlisted the assistance of a prop man, and they discovered an ancient 1929 Flexible Flyer. They wrapped it in green paper with red ribbon like a Christmas present, strapped it to Jack's motorcycle, and drove it to the hospital. He'd been warned that Rock might not recognize him, but as he went in, Rock smiled and immediately reverted to their old swordplay.

"What've you got there?" Rock inquired.

"Where?"

"Right over there."

"Oh, that's a present."

"I wonder who it's for," said Rock.

"Who do you think it's intended for?"

"I'm not sure. "You brought it here."

"It's meant for you, Rock."

"Are you gonna open it?"

Jack unfolded it and placed it on Rock's lap.

"Flexible Flyer," said Rock.

"You and Billy, right?"

"I remember seeing it." He touched the wood's gleaming surface. "Put it against the wall, so I can see it when I wake up."

For the second time since they'd met, Rock took Jack's hand in his.

"Rock, I want you to improve; there are a lot of things we haven't discussed," Jack stated.

"Oh? "How about that?"

"I just want to talk with you."

"What exactly do you want to talk about?"

Jack grinned. It was the same old conversation, and he knew what was going to happen. "Heard any good jokes lately?" he said.

In the summer of 1982, Rock called Mark and George in the desert to inform them that his father's third wife, Edith Scherer, had died. Scherer was 83 years old and senile, and he hadn't recognized his wife had died. A neighbor noticed her reclining on the sofa and realized she wasn't asleep. She dialed 911, who called Rock, who dialed Mark and asked, "What do I do?"

Rock had avoided visiting his father for thirty years, despite paying him fifty dollars every week. "I can't handle it," he told Mark, who replied, as he always did to Rock, "I understand."

Mark arranged for Edith's burial and determined that Scherer should be placed in a home because he was unable to care for himself. Rock and Tom urged him to go to the Motion Picture Country House, which had a huge waiting list for retired actors. There were hundreds of homes in which Rock could have placed his father, and Rock himself had a stake in a Westwood rest home. Rock, on the other hand, insisted on the Motion Picture Country House, so Mark and others had to work favors to get Scherer in. Mark drove Scherer there, but he kept wandering away, and the administration told him they couldn't care for him. Mark addressed Alice Marie, the adoptive daughter of Scherer and his second wife, who lived in Oregon. Mark flew Scherer to Oregon, and a few months later, Alice Marie contacted to say Scherer had died. When Rock was told, he requested ten minutes alone and never addressed it again.

Rock called Stockton Briggle about ten o'clock in the evening in the fall of 1982. "Can I come over?"

"Of course," Stockton responded, despite the fact that he was about to go to bed. Tom was in bed, inebriated, and wanted to talk, according to Rock. Stockton had never heard Rock call like this before and wondered what was bothering him. Rock drove over, they sat up talking, and Rock drank Scotch until Stockton eventually placed Rock in his car at three a.m.

It was a night when Rock unburdened himself of all the worries, torments, and demons he'd been holding inside and suppressing. It is one of the few times in Rock's life that I have found where he confided in someone about his pain. "For some reason, he unburdened himself to me," says Stockton. "I think it stems from the incredible relationship we developed while working on Camelot--the incredible night we spent together reshaping the show." Rock had faith in Stockton and believed that the director understood him.

Rock told Stockton that he felt like a man granted a second chance following his bypass surgery. "It's time for me to make my own decisions and choices." It's time to do what I want without worrying about what other people think." He stated that he despised working in television because everyone settled for too little and that deadlines were more important than quality. "I'm sick of doing nonsense." I'm tired of receiving subpar parts with mediocre scripts." He was resentful that his lengthy years of filmmaking had gone unnoticed and unappreciated.

His mind kept returning to illness and death. He talked about his father, Roy Scherer, and how much he despised him, as well as how much he adored his mother and was saddened when she died. He told Stockton that he couldn't take illness and couldn't accept the truth that his mother wouldn't recover, so he cut himself off from her.

Rock appeared depressed and lonely, so Stockton attempted to reassure him. "Your work is highly regarded by many serious people, and you are adored by millions around the world."

"But no one loves me," remarked Rock.

"You can have Tom."

Scoffing was made by Rock.

"I know Tom loves you."

"There's nothing there anymore," Rock grunted, disgusted. It's strictly social."

Stockton was shaken when Rock departed his residence. "It was an incredible night." Rock was in excruciating pain, and his entire life had been spent trying to mask it. This was similar to Walpurgisnacht, but when I met him again, he never recognized it. I never saw him again like that."

Another unusual trait was Rock's habit of going for walks every day. He'd leave about two, drive somewhere "to walk," and return around six, cheery and whistling, freshly bathed and with his hair still moist. "I bet you he's not going for a walk," James Wright told Mark Miller. He's going to meet someone." "Somehow it always shows," James added later. When you live with someone, you become acquainted with his habits. Mr. Hudson was not the type to go for long hikes. When he returned, he was always cheerful. His eyes were glistening. He'd go directly to the freezer for some vanilla ice cream with chocolate sauce and walnuts. Then he'd go upstairs to his bedroom and begin tatting (needlepointing), while Tom came downstairs to the kitchen and turned on the television. Mr. Hudson disliked television and would not watch it in his bedroom. Mr. Hudson gave me the idea that he'd had enough of Tom."

Rock was out in the afternoons with Marc Christian, whom he met in the fall of 1982. Marc Christian MacGinnis was the sort for whom Rock had a weakness: tall, blond, bisexual, with blue eyes and, when Rock met him, a mustache and beard. He was a "health freak" who went to the gym. He didn't have a regular job, but he claimed Rock he was compiling a history of popular music dating back to the invention of the phonograph.

Rock had a lifelong issue with being unable to face people, fire help, or ask loves to leave. Perhaps he did not want to be in the position of rejecting another person since his father had abandoned him. Instead, he would employ indirect methods. According to Phyllis Gates, "he froze people out." Rock would become silent, nasty, and make the situation so uncomfortable that the person would opt to leave on his own. This strategy, however, did not always work. Rock had been cold to Tom for some time and had left the bedroom, but Tom persisted, assuming that "this too shall pass."

On September 7, 1983, Mark Miller drove Rock and Tom to the airport so they could fly to New York for the autumn. As Tom walked away to handle the luggage, Rock stepped around the side of the van and said to Mark, "I'll be back next Tuesday."

"But . .."

"I won't be going for three months." He is. I'll phone you from New York to let you know about my flight."

"You're on," Mark declared.

Claire Trevor arranged a lavish celebration to welcome Rock and Tom back to New York. They went to attend La Cage aux Folles and discussed Rock's participation in the show with the producers. Rock declared two days later, "I'm going back to California tomorrow."

"We just got here!" exclaimed Tom. "Claire has thrown us this magnificent party. "I'm not going home right now."

Rock stated that he would go nonetheless. Tom had no idea the relationship was over. Rock, he reasoned, was probably hesitant to be away from his doctors and Cedars-Sinai Hospital due to the heart operation. "He had canceled trips at the last minute several times with lame excuses." I reasoned that he didn't want to leave the womb."

On September 13, Mark met Rock at the Los Angeles airport and was disappointed to see him dressed in baggy slacks, an unmatching shirt, and worn, scuffed loafers. "He appeared disheveled, which embarrassed me." I despise seeing a Hollywood star step off a plane looking like shit. "It's bad for his reputation," Mark remarks. When asked about Tom, Rock stated, "I hope he spends the rest of his life in New York." I'll never see him again."

Tom traveled to New York with Claire Trevor on October 27 and stayed at Beresford. Rock flew for Israel four days later to film The Ambassador. Wally Sheft was concerned that Tom would sue for alimony after 10 years with Rock, but Tom stated, "I'm not the suing type." Tom was positive that they will reconcile. "If Rock would just come here and talk to me, we could get our lives straightened out in ten minutes," he remarked. Rock contacted Tom from Jerusalem and said he'd stop in New York on his way home to settle things. Tom waits, but Rock never shows up. He returned to Los Angeles on a direct flight, and Tom did not see him again until Rock was in UCLA Medical Center. Tom began rebuilding his life on his own, but he never gave up. "There was never any doubt in my mind that we'd reconcile."

Chapter 10

One of the worst things in the world is fear. I've felt terrified at times, such as when I was in a car accident, a head-on collision. I remember being so terrified that my hands wouldn't work. A horrible feeling, like an uncontrollable sickness. I dislike things over which I have no control.

The bubble popped within a few weeks of Rock's return from Paris in October 1984. "I've dropped another ten pounds." "What the hell is going on?" Rock said. His face had the wrinkled and droopy appearance of elephant skin. He was sleeping twelve hours a night and fainting for another two hours after lunch. According to Mark Miller, Dr. Sugarman was furious that Rock decided to do Dynasty. He questioned why Rock was putting his health at risk; he might not make it through the show, and he might not see Christmas.

Rock would only listen to Ron Channell at this point. Ron encouraged Rock to have breakfast, which he had never done before, and Rock would nibble at the eggs and toast, only eating half a serving. Rock began wearing only his jockey shorts around the home, and the crew was taken aback by how much his bones protruded. "Mr. Hudson, you need to eat more," John Dobbs exclaimed.

Rock did not speak to James for three days after Mark informed him that he had notified James of his sickness. "He pretended I wasn't there. He couldn't face me because he felt humiliated and ashamed. But then he changed his mind," James says.

Much of the time, Rock was gloomy and silent. "The famous laughter we all love is going," Mark stated. "He'd barely react" when he told Rock stories he knew would make him chuckle. I used to be able to make him laugh no matter how low he was. I used to be able to make him fall to the floor, but not anymore. I was starting to lose him."

Rock began work on Dynasty at the end of October. He'd agreed to perform six episodes, with the possibility of four more and a spinoff series the following year. The cast felt honored to be working with him and were impressed by his politeness to other actors, as well as his unassuming demeanor and sense of humor. Rock entertained audiences with puzzles and anecdotes about great characters such as

David O. Selznick and George Stevens. Rock was advised by John Forsythe to write a book. "You've got all these wonderful stories, you should find a writer to help you put them together."

Rock and Mark Miller had discussed writing a book on numerous occasions but had always determined that the time was not right. When Forsythe brought it up again and again, Rock stated to Mark, "Maybe it's time."

"Okay, let's write the book," Mark said. They sat in Mark's office, on opposite ends of two desks pushed together and facing each other. They took out yellow legal papers and prepared their pencils. They stared at the pads for a few minutes, then glanced at each other and burst out laughing. "That's as far as we got with the book," Mark admits. Forsythe was told by Rock, "I wrote a few paragraphs and made a big decision: no."

When he wasn't on site, Rock joked and spoke with the group, but when he wasn't, he retreated to his trailer and slept. He didn't eat with the cast because he had no appetite and was starting to vomit. When the assistant director came to his trailer to call him for scenes, she had problems rousing him up. She spoke to him, then caressed his arm before rocking and shaking him. "It took a long time for me to figure it out." He was absolutely unconscious."

Rock's memory was deteriorating, so he had to rely on cue cards, which was embarrassing. It meant he couldn't do the most basic component of his job: memorize lines. "His coloring was pale," observed makeup artist Jack Freeman, who had previously worked with Rock. I did everything I could to make him appear better, but it was clear he wasn't feeling well or strong. "Yet his face would light up at times, and he'd look fantastic."

Rock agreed to do the remaining four episodes during his second episode, which aired in January 1985. He completed a total of nine because the story written for his character stopped at the number nine. "I would have kept him forever," Esther Shapiro says. On film, he appeared to be magical. He appeared fatigued at the end of the game, but it was the end of the season. We didn't think he was terribly unwell." Esther claims that if she had known he had AIDS, she would not have hired him. "I would have had to go through the production company and the network." The sick have rights, and so do other actors."

Rock enjoyed his appearance on Dynasty. "Did you see Dynasty last night?" he asked his friends. I believe I present well. "I still look like I did when I first started acting." Rock, on the other hand, was concerned when he heard a script for an episode in which he would have to kiss Linda Evans. He strolled into the kitchen and tossed the script on the table where Mark Miller was sitting. "Christ Jesus. Linda must be kissed. "What am I going to do?" He'd been given the script a week before the shoot, and he'd been agonizing over it all week. The AIDS virus had been cultivated in saliva, according to the press, but there was no evidence that the disease could be transmitted through kissing. Rock did not consult with his own physicians. According to Dr. Gottlieb, "I would not have advised a passionate kissing scene with anyone."

Rock and Mark talked about the kiss and worried about it. "Do I rush over to Gottlieb and Sugarman and say, 'There's a kiss, what should I do?'" Do I tell Linda Evans, Esther Shapiro, and Aaron Spelling?" Rock kept coming to the conclusion that there was nothing he could do. "He was trapped," Mark recalls. "Either you announce you have AIDS or kiss the lady," he reasoned.

I questioned Mark why Rock didn't inform the producers he had a mouth illness and couldn't kiss anyone. "You couldn't suggest that to Rock," Mark added. He'd wave you away, saying, 'It's my kiss, not yours.' He didn't want to ask them to rewrite a screenplay because it would have raised suspicions."

Mark refers to Rock's decision as a "career decision." Rock's career has always come first, with all other considerations coming second. It was the same ruthless, tunnel vision he'd used in all of his life decisions, and it didn't alter. Rock, on the other hand, knows that "way down the line, I'm gonna pay for that kiss." His attitude about the event shifted, and he began putting a pun on the title, Die Nasty.

Mark claims that he, Rock, and George still felt they could keep Rock's illness hidden. "We didn't know there would be an announcement." They discussed transporting Rock to the desert and placing him in a condo with discreet male nurses on call around the clock. "We thought Rock would die slowly and quietly for the rest of his life." Suddenly, there would come an announcement that Rock Hudson had died of liver cirrhosis. We should have known better about Rock; he would die softly."

Rock used every gargle, mouthwash, and spray he could get his hands on on the day the kiss with Linda Evans was filmed. He returned home and told Mark, "The fucking kiss is over." Thank you, God." It was one of the worst days of his life, he claimed.

The episode aired on February 6, and George Nader sat alone in the desert, petrified with fear. He recorded the show, paused it, and then resumed the action. "I could see where Rock kept his lips closed and hit Linda on the side of the cheek for a brief, chaste kiss," he recalls, relieved. No saliva was exchanged since he did not open his mouth."

In retrospect, Esther Shapiro agreed. "There wasn't much of a kiss. Linda loved her husband and was drawing away from Rock, so it couldn't be intense." Esther was not upset when she discovered Rock had AIDS and had not informed the company. "I was horrified to learn that Rock had AIDS and was going to die." She stated that she had not considered the disclosure issue. "The man was ill and wanted to work; he had a long history of denial." "I could understand it."

No one on the Dynasty set seemed bothered by Rock's lack of candor. "She's not worried about getting AIDS," stated a representative for Linda Evans. According to her, medical evidence shows that you cannot contract it by kissing. She is not a worrier; she is a fatalist who believes that everything happens for a reason." Linda Evans spoke at an AIDS event in Los Angeles in September 1985, saying, "Like everyone here, and all his friends around the world, I would like to express my love and support to Rock Hudson."

The cast and crew had become fond of Rock, and their reaction when the news broke was one of sadness. According to one director, "it was a damn shame this had to happen to such a wonderful man." Ironically, no one on the set said what everyone outside was thinking: "How could he have kissed Linda without telling her he had AIDS?" Linda's fans were outraged. "He flat-out exposed her, and I can't forgive him for that," said one man who operates a small business in Los Angeles. I don't believe the physicians who say it can't be transmitted by kissing. They do not yet know everything. Linda should have been informed so she may decide for herself whether or not to incur the risk."

Mark Miller awoke in the middle of the night, concerned that Linda Evans would have AIDS as a result of the kiss. "I shrank from Rock's touch even though I knew he couldn't give it to me by touching." I'd go into the bathroom after he requested me to rub salve on his back and scrub down like a surgeon. On Dynasty, he was rolling on the ground with Linda, kissing her despite the fact that his mouth was closed." Rock, on the other hand, didn't give it another thought until it was over. It was a lifelong pattern: he did not appear to be susceptible to guilt.

In November 1984, when Rock's birthday neared, Mark Miller asked Marc Christian if he wanted to arrange a party. Rock had expressed remorse at losing touch with acquaintances from his youth in the 1950s and 1960s. Rock had ceased seeing folks like Lynn Bowers and Pat Fitzgerald, Bob Garren, Chuck Tilley, Dr. Joe Carberry, Jimmy Dobson, and Wolfgang Bruch once Tom Clark moved in. Tom had brought Rock into a more refined, social crowd, and Rock remarked, "I should never have allowed that."

"Why don't you invite the old-timers, along with his current friends, to a birthday party?" Mark Miller suggested to Christian. They formed a list, and Christian dialed a phone number. He first called Ross Hunter and Jacque Mapes, who indicated they were too busy on Rock's birthday, Saturday. Christian phoned Dean Dittman, who was unavailable, and Jon Epstein, who was also unavailable. He returned to Mark's office and stated, "Everyone's busy on Saturday." "All right, let's change it to Friday," Mark said.

What Mark Miller didn't realize was that Dean was holding a birthday celebration for Rock on Saturday and had invited Ron Channel] rather than Marc Christian at Rock's request. Dean had no idea Mark Miller was organizing Christian's celebration. Christian phoned everyone back, and several of them indicated they were also busy on Friday. Some of the old-timers declined because they had been ignored for ten years and saw this as their chance to retaliate.

Ross Hunter finally dialed Mark Miller's number and informed him of Dean's party. Mark understood he'd made a mistake. "I couldn't tell Christian about Dean's party because Ron Channel] was planning on attending." I had no choice except to let him proceed with the other party." When Mark asked Rock what he should do, Rock replied, "Let him go ahead, I don't care."

Mark Miller missed both parties because he was in the desert over the weekend. He asked Rock, "How'd the parties go?" on Monday, November 19. Rock motioned with his thumbs down. "No sixty-fifth; I'll be leaving town next year."

Rock was coming to terms with what was happening to him and deciding not to fight it. In November, he said that he was done with doctors. He complained that the physicians never called him with the results of his blood tests. "No one calls to say, hey, there's progress or, oh no, there's a setback. Sugarman draws blood, then does nothing. Silence. There can't be any positive news, so why continue sucking the fucking blood? "I've had it--no more blood tests, and that's the end of it!"

Rock had lost interest in sex. Whereas in the past he enjoyed hearing about people's sexual exploits and was delighted when someone delivered him a "care package" of pornography, by the fall of 1984, he didn't want to hear or see anything about sex. "If a sexy scene came on television, Rock would turn it off," explains Dean Dittman. You couldn't talk about sex in front of him; he was dying because he'd had sex."

Mark Miller had the impression that Rock was giving up. "To him, sex and career were the most important things. He couldn't have sex anymore, and his career had dwindled to the point where he was doing a soap opera on TV. He was afraid of the future, therefore he saw a route out and chose to take it."

Rock remained concerned that his condition would "get out in the press." Mark, trying to be lighthearted, stated, "Do you understand that if that happens, you must leave town immediately?"

"But where will I go, sir?" said Rock, feigning naive perplexity.

"To the Yucatan Peninsula or Western Australia." You can spend your days in far-flung corners of the globe."

"You must leave as well, sir." Rock stepped away from the game and stopped smiling. "You're correct. I'm not going to sit here and watch the rejections mount up."

For the first time since arriving in Hollywood in 1948, Rock had spent three nights at home alone. "I had no place to go," he said to Mark. "Ron Channell was busy, and so was Dean." Whereas in previous years, all four lines would ring at all hours of the day and night."Rock loved the phone; he could be talking on one line, holding someone on the other, and if the third line rang, he'd yell, 'I'll get it!'"

Rock sat in Mark's office for extended stretches, staring into space, in the lion's head chair. When Mark was responding to mail or

balancing finances, Rock would say, "I'm gonna die." "I'm going to eat worms," he said, mocking his mother. "I'm going to die."
"No, you're not," Mark responded, impersonating another child.
"I am, too," Rock said.
"No, you're not."
"I am, indeed. "Na na na na na."
"Stop it," Mark would say, and everyone would laugh.
In December, Rock and Dean began learning "Perhaps Love," a duet recorded by Placido Domingo and John Denver, to sing at Christmas gatherings. Rock played John Denver, and Dean played Placido Domingo. Rock enjoyed working on the song, but they were not invited to any events where they could perform, so Rock spent Christmas alone at home. "For Rock, invitations had almost ceased," Dean adds.
They went to Stockton Briggle for a tree-decorating party, and Stockton remembers Rock sitting alone, looking skinny and unhappy, staring wistfully at the tree. Stockton approached him and sat next him, wrapping his arm across Rock's shoulders and holding it there. "He appeared vulnerable, as if he needed help." When Rock left, he apologized to Dean for not being able to share what he had with Stockton. Stockton was saddened to learn this after Rock's passing. Stockton had been told five years ago that he had cancer and would likely die. "I told everyone about it. "I was determined to win, and I did." Rock might have spent his final year surrounded by adoring pals, according to Stockton. "But he had no choice but to tell the world. He preferred to withdraw and die alone."
On Christmas Eve, Rock and Dean attended a party at the home of Martha Raye, Rock's co-star on McMillan, but Rock had to leave early since Tom Clark was due. Dean had toured with Martha in Annie that year, and one night while both were drunk, Dean had slipped and informed her Rock had "the big A." Dean had pledged her to secrecy and was upset with himself for failing to keep it.
When Tom Clark came to the Christmas party, he approached Dean and asked, "What's the matter with our boy?" "You have to tell me if he has AIDS."
"If he has it, I have it, Tom." "No, he couldn't have AIDS," Dean said.
"If he does, I'll be right there, even if he throws me out," Tom promised.

Dean was worried when he watched Tom disappear into a corner with Martha Raye. When Dean returned to his apartment later that night, Tom called and stated, "Martha Raye just told me you told her Rock has AIDS!" Dean denied it, then contacted Martha and insisted that she call Tom and deny it as well; they got into an argument and have been estranged ever since. Tom Clark, on the other hand, claims that he never truly believed it. He didn't find out Rock had AIDS until it was reported in July 1985.

By January 1985, speculations that Rock had AIDS had become increasingly pervasive. "Does he have AIDS?" asked Wally Sheft, who called from New York. "Why don't you ask Rock?" Mark suggested. Wally politely asked Rock the question, and he responded no. "Perhaps I should have told Wally," Rock later reflected. But why is this so? It makes no difference."

As Rock spoke, his hands moved incessantly over his body, scratching, urgently attempting to relieve the itch. He was covered in rashes in his genital area and on his face, and he couldn't use cortisone to relieve them since it would harm his immune system. In his mouth, he had Vincent's disease, and two of his front teeth were loose. He contracted contact impetigo, which was very contagious and left itching sores on his chest, back, and legs. Rock claimed he couldn't sleep at night due to the agonizing itch. He wandered around in jockey shorts since clothing irritated the itching.

One morning after Rock's workout, James entered the bedroom and saw Rock laying on the bed with a thermometer in his mouth. He said to James, "You didn't see this."

Mark and James began a campaign to persuade Rock to return to Paris and be treated by Dr. Dormont once more. Mark showed him a letter from Bob Darcy, a buddy they had sent to Dr. Dormont after Rock had left. (This is a fictitious name; he requested that his real identity be hidden.) Bob had been in Paris for six months and had written that he was gaining weight and swimming two kilometers every day. Doctors in San Francisco warned him he wouldn't live to see his next birthday, yet he was celebrating in Paris!

"It's cold in Paris," said Rock.

Mark stated that he would go first, get an apartment, furnish it, and then Rock could fly in.

"I don't want to hear about Paris!" In Paris, there is no work."

"Forget about your career, you want to live," Mark replied.

"I'm not going to live in Paris alone, and how am I going to explain to Ron that we're going to live in Paris, in the cold?" For what purpose? I can't take Ron away from acting school."
"I did everything to get that man back to Paris," Mark stated after Rock died. He would still be alive today if he had stayed in Paris. Bob Darcy is still alive.

Rock accompanied Ron Channell to Mauna Kea in February for a week's vacation. He lay in the sun for a while, which seemed to help his rashes, but when he returned to the Castle, his weight had dropped to 182. He sat with the employees at lunch and did not eat. If he did, he would excuse himself, walk upstairs, and puke. Nutriment was the only food he could keep down. "I get nauseated just walking through the kitchen," he said.

He spoke and walked slowly, and he frequently struggled to understand simple queries. Under the burden of watching Rock diminish and being forced to lie and cover up, Mark began to shatter. Every Thursday, Mark would go to the desert, sit at the bar, and go into a catatonic slumber. It would take him until Sunday to restore his spirits, after which he would return to the house where Rock was dying, "to Plague Palace, to bell," Mark adds. "However, you were unable to desert. At the very least, I couldn't desert. That's the farm lad from Iowa."

Rock asked Mark if he might come to the desert for a weekend visit in March. Rock had never liked Palm Desert, which shocked Mark. "Sure," he responded, "let's ask George." "Is it okay if I come down?" Rock asked when they contacted George.

"Of course that would be fantastic. Come and bring anybody you want."

"Can't I just come here by myself?" Rock said.

"My God, Rock, sure, just get your ass down here."

They planned an Easter weekend getaway, and on Thursday, April 4, Rock and Mark headed out in Mark's Jeep Wagoneer. George hadn't seen Rock in almost a year, since the weekend he came to see Marc Christian in February 1984. Although George had been informed that Rock looked bad, the sight of Rock's face nonetheless shocked him. It was difficult to believe it was the same face George had known for three decades, the face that had captivated the camera.

George grabbed Rock's hand, wrapped his arms around him, and slapped him on the back. That he could feel the bones beneath Rock's sweater was another surprise. Rock looked George in the eyes and said, "Hiya," making it plain that they were going to be together without pretense. "There were many levels of intimacy Rock and I could use," George adds. We could be quite superficial, staying on the surface and not digging deeper. Rock could go all out and play the movie star, or we could get right down to business and go man-to-man. When Rock said, 'Hiya,' I knew we were on the same page."

The Palm Desert house was low and modern, with windows on all sides facing out on the Bermuda Dunes Country Club's palm trees and beautiful greens, and beyond that, the Palm Springs mountains, which change color throughout the day from tan to salmon to deep purple. George had moved out of the master bedroom for Rock's visit, believing that Rock would be more at ease with a private bathroom nearby.

That night, they ate at the French Quarters, which Mark and George dubbed "the fort" because it had earlier served as General Patton's desert training headquarters. Rock pushed food around his plate and ate a little before asking Mark, "Where's the men's room?"

George raised his eyebrows at Mark. Was Rock going to fall ill? Mark gave a nod.

Rock reappeared ten minutes later, smiling as if he'd only been gone a minute. He showed no signs of being unwell.

The next morning, Rock arrived at the pool in a sloppy pair of old blue shorts. He asked if he might remove his shorts since he had a rash in his groin that the sun would help. Mark and George said it was fine because the land was surrounded by a fence. While George sat in a chaise longue under a shade tree, Rock put a beach towel on the grass and lay down on his back. Because George had skin cancer, he wore pants, a long-sleeved shirt, and a hat. While Mark worked in the kitchen, Rock and George sat in the yard and reminisced about their various dogs through the years. They debated about who was the most intelligent and who was the most charming. Tucker, Rock's first Irish setter, was his favorite, while Matty, a Doberman-Airedale given to him by Rory Calhoun, was George's.

They sat in silence for a time before Rock sighed. "Well, I guess you're right......"

"I'm always right," George declared.

"Like the devil! "You've never been correct." Rock and George had a strong rivalry about who was the wisest over the years, with Rock insisting that he was always right and George was always wrong.

"For once in your life, you're right," remarked Rock. "People are no damn good 99 percent of the time."

George let out a cheer. "What converted you?"

"The phone has gone dead. "I'm at home."

"Are you certain the bill has been paid?"

Rock raised his head and fixed his gaze on George. "No one ever calls... about anything." Ross and Jacque no longer call. My representatives do not contact me. "Not even the fucking doctors call."

"It's no consolation, but that happened a long time ago to Mark and me." When I decided to stop performing. I realize it's not much fun."

Rock stated that he was tired of spending all of his evenings with Dean Dittman and listening to his lectures on God and positive thinking.

"What's the deal with the sleeping prince?" George said, referring to Marc Christian as Rock's nickname. Rock, according to George, responded as follows.

"More of the same." Rock rolled over and lied on his stomach, facing George directly. He smiled solemnly. "You know how he trapped me? He laughed about it afterwards."

"What do you mean, trapped you?"

"Mark, how long till lunch?" Rock yelled as he turned toward the house.

"About ten minutes," screamed Mark.

Rock returned to George and told him that Christian had admitted to him shortly after his return from Israel that he'd taken money for sex. "With that shit-eating grin of his, he said he only did it when he was really so hungry he just had to," Rock imitated Christian's voice. "I told him to get out of here." He simply laughed and continued, "Listen, there's more." It appears that I had been set up--the 'chance' meeting had been planned." Christian had waited for Rock to enter Brooks Baths, according to Rock. "And when I did, he kept waving his dick at me until I realized who he was." The rest, as they say, is history. I still can't believe it, Jesus Christ. Set up and be persuaded by yours truly."

"For God's sake, why didn't you just throw him out?" George stated.

"He said he'd go straight to the Enquirer, that he had a friend who was a reporter, and they were all ready and waiting."

There was an awkward moment. "That ended it for me, for good," Rock added.

George pondered a topic he'd wanted to ask Rock for a long time: why he hadn't told Christian he had AIDS. George sought to determine if this was the right time. "Uh, Rock, when you found out about..."

"Is it the Plague?" I just told you that I was done with Christian for God's sake; we hadn't had sex in months. And if I said anything to him, he'd bolt to Liberty, and she'd have it all over town."

"But . . ." George attempted to express his fear that Christian had been revealed.

"Listen to me." Rock's voice was firm. "You've heard Christian's story. So screw him. It comes with the territory."

They exchanged stares until Mark appeared at the back door. "Lunch, you guys."

Mark and George had planned a trip to Joshua Tree National Park for Saturday. "Yeah! Let's go, let's do it," exclaimed Rock. They got in the Jeep, put on the radio, and drove to the national park, where they planned to do a two-hour circle and eat at the Valley of the Moon restaurant. Rock had never been to Joshua Tree National Park, a desert refuge teeming with exotic cacti, wildflowers, and amazing rock formations. "Goddamn, that's beautiful, look over there!" Rock said. They had arrived at "the cholla gardens," a stretch of desert densely packed with thousands of cholla cactuses, the yellow spines of which glistened in the afternoon sun. They strolled through the cholla, then returned to the Jeep and continued driving.

They soon noticed Joshua trees: big brown and bent yucca plants that appeared to be stuck in the sand like sentries with extended, thorny arms. Patti Page appeared on the local radio station in their automobile, singing "Mockin' Bird Hill." They all burst out laughing, and Mark nearly drove off the road. "Mockin' Bird Hill," even after all these years! It was the tune Rock had repeatedly played in 1951, the song he had loved when they were young and suffering, when they were first starting to know each other. It was the album that Mark and George had vowed to throw out the window if Rock played it again. They laughed till tears streamed down their faces when Mark drove over and stopped.

Then there was silence. Mark started the car, and the two of them drove the rest of the way without saying anything. The sun was setting, and the terrain was as desolate as the moon, but for the Joshua trees, which had spiky arms and strange patterns. "Some other level of communication was taking place," George felt. It was as though the noisy vocal system had to be turned off in order for the wordless to occur." And George knew: Rock had come to say his final goodbyes.

When they reached the park's end, they engaged four-wheel drive and followed a gravel road that seemed to lead nowhere. They could see dim lights in the distance, then clusters of cactus and ocotillo, and ultimately an old stone edifice with the words VALLEY OF THE MOON.

When they walked into the restaurant, the spell was broken. The owner recognized Rock and welcomed him. Platters of farm-style, home-cooked foods were served: fried chicken, mashed potatoes, honey-glazed country biscuits, and Jell-O for dessert. It was the kind of stuff Rock adored, and he ate more than Mark had seen him eat in months. But after the Jell-O, he asked quietly, "Where's the restroom?"

According to George, "it was heartbreaking." They took the shortest path home, sensing Rock's exhaustion.

Rock slept till ten o'clock on Easter Sunday. In the front room, he and Mark needlepointed while George read the newspaper. Mark was chastised by Rock for his "sloppy work," and he showed him where he had made a mistake rounding a bend. "Jeez, it's the easiest thing, any ass could do it."

"Bullshit," Mark exclaimed. "Show it to me."

Rock undid Mark's work, demonstrated the proper stitch, and performed a few rows himself. He then returned to his own piece.

Rock questioned Mark and George's financial situation. "Will you two be okay if something happens to me?" Mark went over what they had and indicated that by living simply, they could get by rather well. They didn't need Rock's money, and he should be free to spend it whatever he pleased.

Mark and George had intended to take Rock to Borrego Springs that day, but George feared Rock wouldn't be able to handle it. "Why don't we just laze around here?" George stated.

"Yeah, I think that's a good idea," answered Rock.

George realized that no extra effort was required. "Rock didn't want or need to be entertained." He was content merely to be with us silently." George was moved that Rock had made a point of coming for this visit, which clearly meant a lot to him. Rock's remarks regarding Marc Christian felt like a final confession to George. "Rock would never have told me those things if he hadn't known it was our last time together." He was too proud to tell anyone, so he kept it to himself."

The fact that this was a farewell visit was never mentioned. "You know, Rock, now that you've lost all that weight, you should get a complete facelift," George stated at one point. Have everything completed."

"Come on!" Under the insistence of a cameraman, Rock had had his eyelids done and thought it was the pinnacle of vanity.

"You've got hollows and lines..."

"Me? Lines? Nah."

"In certain lights, yes." Just a few lines. What the hell, why not have the whole thing pulled up and tightened? It'll look fantastic on TV."

Rock laughed heartily and shook his head. "Thank you, George. "I believe I look like a million dollars."

In May, Mark Miller heard reports that Marc Christian had AIDS and had passed it to Rock. On May 28, when Christian entered his office, Mark asked, "Have you heard the latest rumor about yourself?"

"What exactly is it?" stated Christian.

"That you have AIDS, and you gave it to Rock."

"What! That is absurd." "Does Rock have AIDS?" Christian inquired. Christian had asked Mark the question for the first time.

"Why don't you go ahead and ask him?" Mark stated.

Rock was alone in the kitchen that night when Christian came in and told him the rumor. "Do you have HIV/AIDS?" stated Christian.

Rock gave him a scornful glance. "No. Do you?"

"No," Christian replied. "But something is wrong with you. Why don't you seek assistance? Instead of going to quacks, why don't you go to a good doctor?"

"I'm perfectly fine."

"Have you been checked for cancer?"

"Yes."

"Have you been checked for AIDS?"

"Yes, I've been checked for everything, and I don't have it!" The usual veil fell over Rock's face, masking his expression. In a chilly, menacing tone, he asked Christian, "What would you do if you had it?"

"I'm not sure. "I'd probably kill myself," Christian admitted.

Christian's 1959 Chevy Nomad station wagon caused a commotion in June. Mark Miller had been paying invoices each week for more than eighteen months while the car was being restored at Image Makers. He had totalled up what Rock had invested to date in May-- $20,000--and when advised, Rock answered, "That's it. I'm not going to pay any more." Mark had informed Christian, who had requested more repair done on the car. When a new bill from Image Makers arrived in June for $10,000, Mark informed Christian that he would have to pay it himself.

"Wait a minute," Christian interrupted. "The car isn't finished yet." You can't leave me hanging." Christian claimed that he learned that Image Makers' manager, Mike Frawley, had been inflating the costs because he thought it was Rock Hudson's car. "This individual has charged you for the same part three or four times. He's been stealing from Rock by repeatedly writing up orders for the identical parts. I'm attempting to protect you, and I have all of this evidence. You can't just pull a fast one on me."

"There have been too many problems," Mark stated. We're washing our hands of it."

"If you want me to, I'll just take the car off the lot," Christian said.

"If you can do that without breaking the law," Mark commented.

Margaret Saal, George Nader's attorney, advised Christian on how to get the automobile off the lot without paying the charge. He informed Frawley that Rock wished to have the automobile registered as a vintage vehicle and asked Frawley to join him in the Department of Motor Vehicles. When they drove away from the lot, they came to a stop at a light, and Liberty Martin climbed in. According to Christian, he then "ordered Frawley out of my car." This was legitimate, I discovered, because he knew I was leaving the lot." When Frawley was unable to provide a lien against the vehicle, Christian was permitted to drive it away. "So I took the car to avoid any further expenses," Christian explains.

Mike Frawley claims Christian duped him by repeatedly requesting that work be redone. "At his request, the car was painted twice and upholstered twice." At his request, many of the chrome parts were replaced many times. Because the car is so ancient, there are no new components available; only decent used parts are available. Christian had me go through the paperwork looking for components, and if we found one that was in better shape than one we'd already installed, he had me replace it." Christian, according to Frawley, brought in Liberty Martin's Ford Torino and "told me to fix it and charge the parts to Rock Hudson's company, Mammoth Films, so some of the duplicate parts were for Liberty's car."

When Frawley's payments from Mammoth Films halted, he asked Christian what was wrong. Christian informed him that Rock was dissatisfied with the length of the project and would not pay him again until the automobile was completed. Christian advised Frawley to stop mailing bills to the house, as he would personally handle them. Christian told him that he would be compensated after the job was completed. Frawley directed his crew to labor around the clock to complete the car in three weeks, and he handed Mammoth Films a final cost for $10,000. "I was confident I'd be paid when Christian duped me into driving off the lot with him."

Christian laughed as he informed Mark Miller how he had "liberated" the automobile. "My car is ready, can I bring it up here?" Christian asked Rock. Rock was in the kitchen with Ron Channell, getting ready to begin their workout.

"Definitely not," responded Rock.

"WhY•" ?

"You already know how you obtained it. I don't want those individuals harassing me and following me around."

"I live here as well; this is my house, and this is my car."

"I don't want that fucking car on my property, and that's that!" shouted Rock.

"How can you speak to me like that in front of a servant," Christian exclaimed, pointing to James.

Christian scooped up a chair and flung it across the kitchen as Rock walked out.

When Rock walked out, Ron Channell, who was standing at the kitchen door, remarked, "If I were you, I'd go right back in there and tell that guy to move out."

Marc Christian went into Mark Miller's office, swearing he'd drive his car there whether Rock liked it or not. Mark tapped Rock on the shoulder in the playroom and asked him to come into the office. "Talk it out, guys, come on," Mark said. After some back and forth, Christian and Rock agreed that the car may be parked at the Castle, but it had to be covered at all times.

Meanwhile, James was enraged and informed Mark Miller that he intended to resign. "How dare Marc Christian refer to me as a servant!" He does not own this property. I'm an Englishman with a respectable occupation."

"Listen, straighten out your relationship with Rock," Mark Miller stated to Christian. Go speak with him. You may either fix things out or leave. The house is in commotion, and James is in uproar. Nobody says anything. Rock isn't even talking to you."

That night, when Rock was poking at his food, Christian entered and sat quietly across from him. "Can't we return to what we had two years ago?"

"No," Rock replied. "I don't give a damn about you anymore." In fact, don't bother speaking to me at all. We don't have anything to say. You've put me through hell for the past two years. It's too late now."

Christian's mouth opened wide. Rock returned his attention to his dish, signaling the end of the interview. Christian paused for a while before standing and exiting.

Ron Channell called a meeting with Rock and Mark Miller the next week to address Rock's health. They sat in Mark's office, and Ron made a strong case for action. He wanted Rock to see a new doctor, as well as a dietician and a psychologist. It was time to summon all the powers of science, psychology, and religion to aid in his recovery. While Ron was speaking, Rock sliced through letters with a letter opener. Ron drove ahead, like a coach trying to motivate a squad that was hopelessly behind. "What do you think, men? Shall we do it?"

It was completely quiet. Rock replied, "Let me think about it."

Ron sagged in his seat.

Rock was deteriorating by the day due to a lack of nutrition. He weighed 170 pounds less than before the sickness began, and he appeared to have shrunk. He no longer towered above other guys; he appeared to be a typical stature, around six one. Rock was having nightmares and waking up screaming for the first time in his life. He was sweating so much in his sleep that James had to cover him with plastic sheets. "I stink at night," Rock said to Mark Miller. "What is that horrible odor?"

On July 5, Dean called to report that Ross Hunter had informed him that "I hear Rock's being drugged by the staff." Mark mentioned this again to Rock, who replied, "Yes, and I wish you'd stop it."

On July 15, Rock decided to go to Carmel to tape a performance with Doris Day for her new cable show, Doris Day's Best Friends. A press conference had been scheduled, and Life magazine was planning to photograph a possible cover photo of Rock Hudson and Doris Day. Mark tried to urge Rock not to attend, as did the physicians and Dale Olson, but it was futile. "I don't think Rock realizes the change in his appearance," Mark told them.

Rock left for Carmel on Monday, "hanging by a thread," and Mark took an executive decision the next day: Rock was returning to Paris. He made plans for Rock and Dean to leave on Saturday and asked Dr. Gottlieb to notify Dr. Dormont in Paris. Mark called Wally Sheft and informed him that Rock was traveling to Geneva for anorexia treatment. Mark did not tell Wally that Rock had AIDS until Rock collapsed in Paris.

Rock appeared late for the press briefing in Carmel, dressed in mismatched, baggy clothes. When it was over, the reporters gathered around Dale Olson, visibly terrified. "What's the matter with Rock?" He was scarcely lucid."

"He's had the flu," Dale explained. "I was afraid that we'd have to cancel."

"It looks even worse than that," one reporter observed.

"No, I don't think so," Dale responded.

U.S.A. Today featured a photo of Rock and Doris, and Dale began receiving calls from all around the world. "Is Rock dying?" Tom Clark called Dean and expressed concern over the photograph. "The whole town is buzzing." Liz Smith said that Rock was in the hospital, and people contacted to inquire about where to bring flowers.

Doris Day and her son, Terry Melcher, were so worried about the shoot that they tried to call it off, but Rock was anxious that it would go forward. On Tuesday, July 16, they began filming, and that evening, after supper, Rock asked Dale to his room. "I've ordered some drinks, please come and talk to me," Rock remarked. Dale discovered Rock on the bed of the suite, with a fire going, music playing, and four Scotches and four vodkas on the table.

"When you order drinks, you just order drinks," Dale explained.

"Well, they take a long time to get here, so I thought I'd order a bunch."

Dale realized it would be a long night. "I spent a lot of time around Judy Garland," he says. Dale states. "She was so afraid of being alone that you couldn't leave until she passed out." That's how I felt about Rock that night." "I'd better go, you've got to sleep," Dale kept saying, and Rock responded, "No, no, don't leave."

Rock wanted to talk about personal issues, something he had never spoken with Dale. He talked about those, who had been genuine friends to him and who had not. Dale recalls being astonished that some of the people he assumed were Rock's buddies were not.

"You know, the most important person who ever was in my life was Tom Clark," Rock stated. "Tom could make you laugh, and he was a joy to travel with." He was devoted and made the house sing. He was fantastic."

"Really," Dale replied.

Rock admitted that his life had fallen apart since Tom's death. The music was no longer alive. He had sincerely loved Tom but had no idea how much.

"Maybe you should see him again."

"No, I don't believe so." I'd like to, but I'm not sure."

Marc Christian was not mentioned by Rock. Rock had asked Dale two years ago whether he might assist Marc with his music project. Rock had proudly shown him the recordings Marc was gathering on pop music history. Dale had told Rock a few months later that he had some ideas for obtaining an institution to support Marc's research, but Rock had dismissed him. "Don't even bother." It won't come to that."

Dale was a lifelong friend of Shirley MacLaine, so Rock inquired about her. Dale revealed that she was working on a television show on reincarnation. Rock was fascinated; he admitted that he didn't believe in God, at least not in the sense that God was commonly portrayed, but he did believe in reincarnation, saying, "I think there's truth to that."

Dale announced his departure at three o'clock in the morning. "You need to get some sleep, Rock, or I'll cancel the shoot." You can't go in front of the camera if you haven't slept. You're not going to do that to Doris." Dale went to bed, and when his alarm went off, Rock was already up, shaving and ready to go.

Doris Day's Best Friends was presented on the Christian Broadcast Network shortly after Rock's death, and it is a moving little film. Doris and Rock appear on a split screen, like they did in Pillow Ta/k. Doris is in her living room, filling a vase with flowers. She dials a number, and Rock, on the other side of the screen, answers.

"I love my roses," Doris sings more than she speaks.

"All ok... good. Beautiful roses for a lovely blonde." Rock is laidback and folksy, and you can feel the warmth through the television. Doris is overjoyed that he will be the first guest on her show. He says he'll take the first available flight up. She claims there is an issue. "Because we're on a tight budget, could you take the bus?"

Music begins, and we see Doris waiting for a rickety old white bus on a country lane. "Here comes the camel," she cries. Doris and Rock are almost the same age, yet the disparity between them is breathtaking. She bounces up and down with spring and vigor, whereas he steps off the bus slowly and stiffly.

"Give me a hug," Rock requests.

"Ohhhh, I haven't seen you," Doris replies, clutching her.

They drive to her house in an ancient yellow convertible. As they go about the grounds and gardens, she sings "My Buddy," pausing to admire a tree or throw a stick for a dog. Doris with her bouncing step and Rock shambling beside her, his hands in his pockets, they look so at ease. One of her dogs flops at Rock's feet as they sit on the terrace.

Doris asks, "Did he get tired?"

"No, I did," Rock responds.

"I gave you a good tour," Doris says. "I miss those belly laughs we used to have."

"I do as well. I haven't laughed like that in a long time."

"We had a lot of fun making movies."

"I wish we'd made more," says Rock.

"We should do it again."

Doris encourages him to stay for dinner, but Rock declines because he has a bus to catch. A final hug occurs at the bus stop, and Rock kisses her on the lips while keeping his mouth closed. As the white bus rattles away, she sings, "My Buddy..."

"When we were walking around out there together, it crossed my mind that it might be the last time," Doris recounted afterwards. But I didn't know for sure. I hoped and prayed that it would not be the case. I didn't know what was wrong with him, but I knew he was going to do that program until he died. It was his final act, and it was with me, which I treasure."

Doris forced Rock to vow to eat more. Rock slept the entire flight to Los Angeles, but in the midst of the flight, he opened his eyes and stared at Dale. "I'm thinking about going to Paris."

"Oh, why?"

"Doris is upset with me. I need to see a doctor in Paris because I think there's something wrong with me. I don't like the fact that Doris is upset with me." He closed his eyes and fell asleep.

Mark's thoughts kept returning to a conversation he'd had with Rock the month before after Mark and George had placed Rock on the aircraft to Paris, in the brief intermission before the sky collapsed in. Mark had learnt more from Rock in that ten-minute conversation than he had in the previous thirty-four years, and he was still processing it in his head, plumbing it.

On a calm afternoon in the house, Rock and Mark were sitting in the office. "Let's take a walk," Rock said. He stood up and extended his arm to Mark, signaling that it was time to "practice our bows." Mark hooked his arm around Rock's, and they strolled out to the deck, where they could chat privately and without being overheard.

They walked around pretending to be noblemen in velvet clothes.

"Do you think the queen is still in the palace?" Rock said.

"The countess is here, I saw her carriage."

They marched across the patio, past the pool and fountains, and onto the deck, heads held high. They rested at the railing, staring down on the citrus and rose terraces and the misty metropolis below. There was no sound but the twittering of birds.

Rock stated that he was eager to get started on the book. "It's that time."

"I completely agree with you there."

"What the hell do we put in a book?" says the author. Rock said.

"For starters, who have you loved? We're talking about true love here, not infatuations or fucks."

119

"Only two people," Rock explained. "Phyllis Gates" and "Lee Garlington."

Mark was intrigued; it was not the answer he expected.

"Lee just drove me crazy," Rock admitted.

"I knew that at the time, although...'

"You didn't like him, did you?"

"No, I found him supercilious."

"He led me on a merry chase," Rock explained. "Goddamn it, I loved him."

Lee Garlington was taken aback when he learned what Rock had stated months later. "I had no idea Rock cared to that extent." When told, Phyllis Gates responded swiftly, "He was telling the truth. Rock never had feelings for me. He didn't seem like a good guy to me."

Mark Miller was hesitant to confront Rock. "He opened up so little that when he did, you simply took what he gave you and didn't press." Mark just stated, "None else?"

No, said Rock, shaking his head. "Those are the only people I've ever truly loved." I thought I accomplished the rest, but I didn't. I recognized I didn't love them soon after I got into the position. It wasn't love; it was sex or infatuation. Then I had to figure out how to get them off my property."

"How come you can't say those two words: get out?" Mark stated.

Rock burst out laughing. "I don't know, but I can't."

Rock stepped away from the railing and extended his arm. "Shall we?" The two guys resumed their regal position and strolled back across the width of red tile, occasionally bowing.

Chapter 11

I have no acting philosophy or anything else. You simply do it. And I really mean it. You simply do it. However, after 35 years, I can say that with confidence. "Just do it," you say to a beginner, and it doesn't imply dits, does it? You must complete the large circle in order to return and remark, "You just do it."

Someone once asked me what my life philosophy was, and I responded something ridiculous. How the heck do I know? I should have said.

On July 30, 1985, Rock was transported home from Paris on a chartered 747 and helicopter to UCLA Medical Center. "Should he see friends?" Dr. Gottlieb asked Mark Miller the next day when he arrived. Dr. Gottlieb agreed that Rock should visit as many people as possible in order for him to want to come back to life.

Mark drew up a list of visitors, and everyone except Marc Christian and Tom Clark was approved by Rock. Mark hired a guard and private nurses to keep an eye on Rock, and the hospital built a visitor area next to his room. Mark would schedule one morning and one afternoon visitor. He called them up and gave them a speech: Rock doesn't look like we remember him, so try not to be surprised; he may not know you or speak, so you'll have to do the talking; and don't stay too long. The guests would walk into the lounge after the visit and "fall apart," according to Mark. Dr. Gottlieb made himself available to address queries from celebrities such as Elizabeth Taylor and Carol Burnett.

On August 8, Juliet Prowse arrived at Rock's house, and when she learned he hadn't seen Tom Clark, she asked, "Would you like to see Tom?"

"Sure," Rock replied.

She informed Mark Miller, who went to ask Rock, and when Rock said yes, Mark contacted Tom. "Get over here right now."

Tom drove to the hospital with Jon Epstein, who was due to arrive at 1 p.m. "I was shaking like a leaf," recounts Tom. Jon and Mark jumped in first, followed by Tom a few minutes later. Rock's face brightened.

"How you doin', pal?" Tom stated.

"Pretty good," replied Rock. He then smiled. "It's a pain, isn't it?" The shitholes."

Little was said, but Tom knew from Rock's eyes and voice, "It was all right between us." I walked into that room and bingo. It seemed as if I'd never left. And guess what? I thought he was lovely. I expected him to look worse because of the Doris Day photos, but he looked fantastic."

Jon Epstein and Mark both left to give them space, and Mark remembers, "It was terribly touching." I hadn't seen Rock smile so broadly since he'd collapsed. His expression seemed to say, "Thank God you're here, buddy, I need you."

Tom literally moved in and took over Mark's duties at the hospital. He'd arrive at eight o'clock in the morning and leave at nine o'clock at night. He read to Rock, sat with him while watching TV, and cajoled and tormented him into eating. "Now, eat your mashed potatoes," Tom would instruct. "How are you going to get better if you only weigh two pounds?"

"All right, then, I'll eat!" Rock said.

Tom scheduled visits and delivered the speech, adding, "He has no idea about the AIDS hoopla." Don't bring it up." Someone did, however, slip and inform Rock that he was on the cover of Newsweek. "Why am I on the front cover?" Mark was questioned by Rock.

"Because everyone loves you," remarked Mark.

Within two weeks, twenty-eight thousand letters had arrived at Rock's hospital or home, some simply addressed to "Rock Hudson, Hollywood." Fans donated Bibles, handcrafted presents, and sweets; church members constructed scrolls and penned small comments expressing their love and congratulating Rock on his bravery. Among the gifts was a button with the words I LOVE ROCK in red letters and a heart in place of love. Tom wore it on his shirt and never removed it.

Rock was calling Tom "Babe," as he had done in previous years, and appeared to be thinking Tom would accompany him home. "I have to hear Rock say he wants you in the house," Mark explained. I want to make certain that I am only acting in accordance with Rock's desires." So, in the sight of Mark, Tom asked Rock, "Is it okay if I come home?"

"Well, of course," Rock responded.

Later, when they were alone, Mark informed Tom that he was not in Rock's will and that Rock was too unwell to make any changes. "So, if you're doing this with the hope of being reinstated, that's not going to happen." You must determine whether or not to continue nursing an AIDS patient."

Tom stated that he didn't care about AIDS or the will because he was grateful for this time with Rock. "I would have been desolate if he had died in Paris and I hadn't been able to be with him again."

The day after Rock returned to California, Christian flew to Paris. Bob Darcy greeted Christian at the airport, assisted him in finding a place to stay, and drove him to Percy Hospital, where he was evaluated by Dr. Dormont. Christian traveled to the south of France with Darcy while awaiting the results of his blood culture. Christian was impressed that Darcy appeared to be in good health. They stayed together in Mougins, a small village outside of Cannes, and went to the beach during the day and to a gay bar called Zanzi at night. "All the Europeans were scared of Americans," Darcy says. "When they heard the accent, they'd say, 'You all have AIDS,' and they'd walk away." Darcy was taken aback by the fact that Christian "didn't seem all that freaked out." I would have been terrified. He appeared to be more worried with Rock than with himself." "Rock was one of the nicest, most generous people I ever knew," Darcy added, "but I was angry he hadn't told Marc he had AIDS." Marc didn't seem angry, which surprised me. My rage was greater than Marc's."

Dr. Dormont reported on August 7 that Christian's culture was negative, with no AIDS virus in his blood and no antibodies to the virus. When the staff at the Castle heard the news, they leapt up and down and hugged each other. Christian returned from France a few days later.

Wally Sheft called Mark Miller from New York on August 12 and stated he, Rock, and Dr. Gottlieb had discussed it and determined that Christian should leave the house before Rock was returned home since his presence might bother Rock. Mark called Christian and asked him to meet him at the Castle at six o'clock. Mark requested James' presence because he needed a witness other than George. The four of them sat in the huge living room.

"Rock wants you to move out of the house," Mark Miller remarked. "Why is he afraid of publicity?" stated Christian.

"No, he just wants you to leave." These are his final days, and that's exactly what he wants."
"Why doesn't he tell me himself?"
"He doesn't want to speak with you."
"I just don't believe it." Christian's voice started to raise. "How can I be sure you're telling me the truth?" For a year, you lied to me! Why should I accept what you're saying now if I wasn't told about AIDS? I'm not required to leave this house. This is my residence. It's not yet your home!"
"That's it," George said to Mark. You were the one who delivered the message. Let's get started." He and Mark began heading out, but as they approached the bar, Christian yelled, "You're trying to kill Rock, Dr. Gottlieb is trying to kill Rock." I could have convinced Rock to return to Paris for more of the drug, but you couldn't." George held Mark in front of him, detecting Christian's attempt to agitate him. Mark shifted his weight. "I tried to help you, I did everything I could..."
"You tried to murder me!" exclaimed Christian.
They departed as George pushed Mark toward the door.
Christian claims he never accused anyone of attempting to kill Rock or himself. He was upset because "I was told a different story every day about why I had not been informed about AIDS." "Let me tell you something that's been kept from you," Mark Miller kept saying. I wasn't supposed to tell you. Rock made the decision, not me. For the past year and a half, I've been carrying out Rock's commands." Christian was so frustrated that he decided to visit an attorney, Marvin Mitchelson, who specialized in palimony cases.
Mark Miller informed Rock that Christian refused to go unless Rock personally asked him to. "Fuck him!" says one. Rock waved his hand dismissively. But Mark persisted, and Rock eventually consented to see Christian. Mark drove Christian to UCLA, took him to Rock's room, and then strolled out into the hall, where he waited with Tom Clark and Tammy Neu, the private nurse. Mark could see Christian standing at the foot of Rock's bed through the open door, but he couldn't hear what they were saying. Christian stepped out of the room after only five minutes. "Did he ask you to leave?" Mark stated.

"No, I had to ask him--do you want me to go?" He agreed. So I said, "All right, I'll leave." "All I need is some time to look for an apartment."

"Isn't that typical of Rock?" Mark asked. Even on his deathbed, he couldn't pronounce the words."

Tom Clark and Tammy Neu corroborated that when Christian left Rock's room, he indicated that Rock had requested him to leave. Christian's closest ally in the house, John Dobbs, claims Christian told him the next day that Rock had requested him to leave.

However, when Christian filed a lawsuit against Hudson's estate, he stated, "Rock never asked me to move out." His account of the hospital room conversation is as follows: Hudson inquired about the house and the dogs. "Why didn't you tell me you were sick?" Christian said.

"When you've got a disease like this, you're all alone."

"I would not have fled from you." I did not flee my father's cancer. I would have been glad to assist you." "Do you want me to move out?" Christian then asked Rock.

"No, why would you do something like that?" Rock said. "Carry on as usual."

Mark Miller found out on August 24 that Christian had gone to meet Marvin Mitchelson. Christian informed Mark that he had no intention of suing, but that he believed he deserved compensation for being exposed to AIDS and had gone to "find out my rights." "Trust me, you'll be taken care of in some way," Mark added. You should not take this to court. It will injure both Rock and you."

"No way," Christian responded.

Mark informed him that they would be transporting Rock home that night, and that Tom and a nurse would accompany him and would need to use Tijuana. Christian announced that he was leaving that day and would be gone before Rock arrived. He put his belongings in boxes in the playroom.

Rock had yearned to see the Castle with every breath he took. "Right out that window and up the hill is home," he insisted. Mark and Tom had planned to take Rock out of the hospital around three a.m. to avoid being followed by the press. Mark and Tom enjoyed dinner at Matteo's in Westwood on Saturday night, then contacted James to see if Christian had left. James stated that he had left and that everything was OK. At nine a.m., Mark and Tom returned to the hospital and asked the chief of security whether there were any reporters downstairs. He declined. "Let's go right now," Tom suggested. They put Rock in a wheelchair with his pajamas and robe, and Tom pushed the wheelchair down the halls and out a back exit, flanked by guards. They climbed into Rock's new Mercedes, with Rock sitting in the back with Toni Phillips, the nurse, and Mark sitting in front with Tom, who began driving down Sunset. Tom was perspiring and his hands were trembling. "Relax, nobody's following us," Mark assured them.

"Why are you driving so fast?" Rock said.

"I'm not driving fast; I'm going 25 miles per hour." "Shut up," Tom instructed.

Mark laughed to himself. "We were transported back in time ten years."

They got to the Castle and assisted Rock in entering through the first front entrance. Rock sat on the wooden bench after the dogs ran up and pounced on him. "Hello there, Bozer, Sister, Casey!" Then he walked slowly across the red-tile patio. James emerged from the kitchen and paused at the entrance, attempting to keep his emotions in check.

"There's James," Tom pointed out.

"Hello, James!"

They entered through the second front entrance, and Tom grabbed Rock's arm and stated, "We go to the right..."

"I understand! I understand!" "Am I not allowed to look at my house?" Rock wished he could stand and stare in every direction, resolving the details in his head. He climbed up the stairs and paused on the landing to gaze down at the red room: the big Pillow Talk couches, the giant candles flickering in parchment shades, the tree limb ceiling. Rock eventually entered his bedroom and climbed into the bed with the winged and crowned masculine image on the headboard. "It was wonderful to see him in his bed," Mark says. He'd gone full circle, halfway around the world and back, for a quarter-million dollars." Mark offered a silent prayer of thanks and drove back to the desert, thinking everything was settled.

The next morning, James was in Rock's room with the nurse when he noticed the light on the desk phone turn on. When James entered the kitchen, he noticed Tom watching a football game on television.

"Who's the one on the phone?" James stated. "Mr. Hudson isn't, neither is the nurse, nor are you."

"I honestly don't know."

"It's a line used by Marc Christian. Allow me to investigate the playroom."

James reappeared two minutes later. "He's made a comeback."

"You're joking," Tom replied.

"No, he's in the kids' room." He crept back into the house last night without notifying anyone. He's sleeping on the sofa bed, and his belongings are scattered across the room. He even hung posters on the walls."

Christian later revealed that he had been unable to obtain an apartment. Tom contacted Mark Miller in the desert, who contacted Wally Sheft in New York, who checked his solicitors and determined that, due to California residence requirements, Christian would have to leave voluntarily, or Rock would have to sign an affidavit and have the marshal evict him. Rock's counsel urged that they ignore Christian and leave him in the house. Wally asked Mark and George whether they would be willing to relocate to Los Angeles to oversee the Castle during Rock's final weeks.

"It was a mess," James admits. "Both Tom and Christian were present in the house at the same time, and I was caught in the middle." According to James, Christian had a buddy stay with him in the playroom almost every night, "sleeping with him in the same bloody bed while Mr. Hudson was lying up there dying." Christian claims that he had friends remain with him because "I was afraid I might be poisoned."

Tom didn't want Rock to know Christian was still in the house, so he avoided bringing Rock downstairs when Christian was present. When they met in the kitchen, Tom was polite to Christian. "I decided I couldn't deal with anything but what's going on upstairs," Tom explained. "All of my energy is going up there, and I'm not going to waste it."

Mark Miller called a staff meeting on Monday, August 26. He stated that Wally had put him in charge of the house and that he and George would be spending four nights a week in their Hollywood condo and coming to the desert on weekends. "Tom, you're in charge of the patient," Mark pointed out. "James will run the house, and I'll disburse the money." Tom was not to order the personnel around;

James had made it clear that one order from Tom would result in his resignation. Marc Christian was free to do anything he pleased. "I'll ask Rock every day if he'll see you." Ron Channel was to have unlimited access to Rock.

Every day, Ron Channel] would walk in wearing shorts and a tank top, and Rock would always smile when he saw him. "Ron was now in the position Jack Coates had previously held--the knight who could jump to the throne at will," Mark recalls. Mark was asked by Ron Channell if Rock would pay for him to take dancing classes so he could perform in Las Vegas. "Rock has always said that he'd help me with my career," Ron explained. "Let's go ask him," Mark suggested, and Rock agreed, "sure, why not."

Tom was on duty at the Castle 24 hours a day, terrified that something might happen to Rock if he left, although he went to his condo once a week to pick up mail. Mark and George went up to Rock's room one day when he was gone and sat on the blue ottomans facing the bed. "You should know what's going on in your house," Mark pointed out. "We want to tell you because it's been kept from you for years."

"I wish you would," said Rock.

Mark informed him that Christian was still in the Castle, resting on the playroom sofa bed. The news didn't seem to bother Rock; rather, "a secret twinkle came to his eyes--they darted around the room as he thought about the situation," George adds. Rock adored mystery, and I think he enjoyed imagining Tom in Tijuana and Christian in the playroom. "Has Christian gotten a job yet?" Rock said.

"I don't believe so. "Would you like to see him?"

"No, fuck him," said Rock. "When's Ron Channel] coming by?"

"He'll be here at five-thirty."

Mark and George also wanted to tell Rock what had happened as a result of his AIDS revelation. "We wanted him to know what he'd done for the world before he became too far gone to comprehend it." George began by saying, "Rock, you're a hero around the world, and the world loves you."

"You're the biggest thing since the pay toilet," Mark declared. "You're ten times more popular than you were ever as a movie star."

"Why? "I have done nothing."

"The announcement that you have AIDS stunned the world," Mark explained. "You've made AIDS the front-page story in every newspaper and the front of every magazine. You've brought the disease to life; the entire world is aware of AIDS because of you."

"You're joking."

Thousands of people, according to Mark, are donating money to AIDS research, and governments are allocating significant funding. After Rock's announcement, the AIDS dinner that Elizabeth Taylor was trying to organize in Los Angeles had to be relocated to a larger ballroom. "They'd sold 200 tickets before your announcement. They've now sold twenty-five hundred and raised a million dollars."

"And all because I said I had AIDS?"

Rock Hudson was the first well-known person to develop the sickness, according to George, and if it could happen to him, it could happen to anyone. "Downstairs, we have thirty thousand letters." You're getting more letters and publicity today than you have in your whole acting career of sixty-two pictures."

Rock rolled onto his side, resting his head on his elbow. "Isn't that cool?"

"Wouldn't you know Rock was gonna be immortal?" Mark asked George.

"We've made you a Goddess," George laughed. It was a private joke based on a passage from Claudius.

"Please, God," Rock begged.

The three began to cry; Mark and George felt they had to leave or they would cry, and Rock was crying despite himself. It was nearly beyond his comprehension: the exact thing he'd been resisting with all his might had happened, and it had only brought good. Mark and George shook his hand and patted him on the back before going downstairs and breaking.

When the Santa Ana wind began to blow and the weather became hot and dry in September, Tom remarked to Rock, "Let's go sit on the deck, there's a full moon tonight-it's your favorite kind of night." Tom led Rock outside and sat him down on a chair. The wind had removed all of the contaminants from the air, and the vista was breathtaking. They could see all the way to the Palm Springs mountains, where the jets turned on their landing lights and began their steady descent over Los Angeles International Airport.

Rock and Tom talked about their travels, and Tom received the impression Rock wanted to talk about death. "I wouldn't let him because I knew he wasn't going to die." I probably let him down, but I didn't want to think about it."

"You're not fighting this, Rock," Tom murmured gently as they sat in the warm, blowing air. You and I have fought and won some major wars. "Are you willing to fight with me?"

"No, I don't think so," responded Rock.

"Y• "I'm ready."

"Well, I'm not sure I'm ready for you to leave."

"See that plane?" Rock said. "We're on it coming back from Rio de Janeiro." They talked about their trip to Rio and how they had danced in samba lines in the street, and then they pointed to other planes and talked about other trips they had taken, to Japan, Australia, Sicily, and Hawaii. After an hour, Rock expressed his tiredness and desire to sleep.

"We had some fun in the house those last few weeks," Tom says. "If you weren't such a chicken," Rock observed one night, "you'd get out a deck of cards and play Spite and Malice." Rock and Tom played cards and thrashed each other, "and we swore at each other-'You dirty prick!' just like we'd always done."

Every morning at six o'clock, Tom would come into Rock's room to see how he'd slept, drink coffee with him, and read the newspaper while Rock worked on the crossword problem. Tom turned on The $25,000 Pyramid at nine o'clock. When Tom left in 1983, Rock exclaimed, "Thank God, we don't have to see the fucking Pyramid anymore," but when Tom returned, the Pyramid was turned back on. They watched movies on cassette and cable, but Tom was hesitant to turn on network television because the Enquirer was airing advertising pushing Rock and Linda Evans tales.

Tom's birthday was September 6, and when he got to Rock's room that morning, Rock was standing between two nurses, holding a cake and singing "Happy Birthday." Tom was touched that Rock, despite his illness, remembered the day and planned a party.

Friends arrived at the Castle in droves, bringing pies and cakes, souffles and soups. It was exhausting for Rock to see visitors, but when Tom placed his palm on his shoulder as he lay with his eyes closed and murmured, "Elizabeth is here," Rock grinned. "Oh, that's good."

Joy arrived one day with a pot of gizzards, but Rock couldn't eat them. "Your name is sure to be on everyone's lips," Joy added.

"Speaking of coming out of the closet... You exited the home!" Rock burst out laughing. "And you're also doing a lot of good." Joy and Rock discussed how they had argued over the crossword problem and who had won. "You sure loved the dogs," replied Rock.

"I did, and you're somewhere in there between those seven dogs."

Rock began having days when his thoughts would cloud and just walking to the bathroom would tire him by the third week he was home. When George attempted to massage his shoulders, he felt nothing but bones because he weighed 140 pounds. For days, Rock couldn't get out of bed, but then he'd get up, wander down to the kitchen on his own, and entertain visitors.

On September 11, George and I went into Rock's bedroom to do an interview. The enormous bed was turned up to eleven, and Rock was seated in his blue pajamas beneath a navy comforter. Closed, the dark wooden shutters filled the room with the strongly fragrant aroma of ginger, which Clarence had sliced and placed in a vase.

Rock had been watching the film Blood and Sand, starring Tyrone Power. "Now here comes one of your all-time favorites, The Postman Always Rings Twice, starring Lana Turner," Tom added. Rock sighed and gazed at the TV, saying, "Lana Lana Lana."

Lester Luther, the voice coach who taught George to lower his voice, was mentioned by George. "I went out in the hills and yelled," said Rock. He remained mute. "I didn't have any, shoot." He appeared perplexed. "I don't recall. "I honestly don't remember."

George tried once again. He inquired about Rock's acting coach, a lady.

"She was just terrible!" Rock said.

I chuckled partially because of how he said it--like a toddler calling the instructor stupid--and partly because I felt uncomfortable. Rock's face brightened.

"She was so dumb!"

George and I were both laughing now, and Rock moved around in his bed, enjoying the noises he was making. His eyes focused and he repeated it, "She's so dumb!" while we laughed even more. His face was bright with color, and he appeared to be content.

When the house was silent and everyone had gone, Tom would climb into bed with Rock and clasp his hand. "Sometimes he'd clutch my hand, sometimes he wouldn't," Tom explains. "I'm sure he got what I was saying. I'd chat and talk, saying encouraging things and reassuring him that he wasn't alone."

Everyone admired Tom for his concern for Rock. According to Stockton Briggle, "Tom was selfless; he had nothing to gain, he'd been cut out of the will, and he might have been risking his health by being so close to an AIDS patient." Tom accompanied Rock to the toilet and into the shower, where he bathed himself rather than having the nurses do it. "I'm so glad to see you back to help him in his final days," Clarence stated to Tom. "A man can ask for and do nothing more."

Tom was alone in the house with Rock and one of the nurses on Saturday, September 21. Rock received a blood transfusion but did not respond well and was being fed intravenously. The doorbell went off. When Tom opened the door, he was greeted by a tall, well-dressed woman clutching a Bible. "I've come to bring Mr. Hudson a message from God," she explained.

"That's just not possible," Tom explained.

"It has to be possible because God told me I'd see Mr. Hudson." Would you mind if I waited here because I know I'll see him?"

Tom shut the door, went to make his lunch, ate it, and returned to the door to find the woman still there. "I'm sorry, lady, but you'll have to leave the premises."

"OK, OK. I'll wait outside the gate since I'm sure I'll see him."

"There was Rock and he looked so sick," Tom recounts, "so I came down and got the lady and brought her up." I can't tell you how out of character that is for me! I often throw nuts off the property." "Mr. Hudson," the woman continued as she stood at the foot of the bed, "I have come with a message from God."

Rock grinned at her as he opened his eyes.

"God has asked me to inform you that you will not be leaving us just yet." He has a ministry here on earth for you that will be far more rewarding than your film career. The cancer will leave your body, and you will be healthy."

Tom led her downstairs and discovered her name was Eleanor. "Now I can tell you about my day," she announced. Eleanor stated that she prays to the Lord and that he sometimes responds. "I was praying this morning when the Lord said, 'I want you to go see Rock Hudson and take him a message.'" 'I can't do that, I'm too bashful,' I answered. "The Lord said, 'Yes, you can and will.'" Eleanor had read

132

that Rock was at UCLA and drove there to find out he'd been discharged. She went back in her car and was driving down Sunset when she noticed a man selling maps to the homes of Hollywood celebrities. She purchased one, but Rock's house was not on it. "'I tried, you see, I tried, and I can't,' I told the Lord. 'Yes, you can,' responded the Lord. Do it.' " Eleanor found Pat Boone's residence on the map and drove there because she knew Boone was devout. Shirley Boone knocked, and when Eleanor explained why she'd come, Shirley "nearly fainted." Right there in the house, they were having a prayer vigil for Rock Hudson." Shirley said she'd find out where Rock lived and gave Eleanor the information a few minutes later.

Tom was still surprised that he'd brought her in. "I think the Lord made me do it," he confessed. "Could I hug you?" Eleanor said, and they hugged and cried.

The next day, Sunday, the actress Susan Stafford called to say the Boones had been holding a 24-hour prayer vigil for Rock and invited her to come lay hands on him. Susan, a born-again Christian and intern preacher, had been a friend of Rock's since 1970. "I figured they couldn't hurt," Tom explains. The group was in Rock's bedroom fifteen minutes later, kneeling around the wooden bed with their hands on the sheet. While Rock slept, Shirley Boone led the prayers. "Rock, there are a lot of good friends here," Tom commented when they were finished. I'd like you to thank them." Rock awoke, muttered, "Thank you," and went back to sleep.

Many of Rock's friends were outraged when they found that born-again Christians could pray over him, saying, "Rock would never have stood for that if he'd been conscious." "I never heard him say anything for or against religion," Tom added. I'll do everything; I'll battle and fight and refuse to give up. If you know a witch doctor, I'll have one here." Mark Miller had asked Rock what religion he practiced the previous year, and Rock had replied, "I guess, Congregationalist." But, according to Tom, Rock was baptized a Catholic and had chosen a Catholic service for his mother when she died. Tom determined that Rock should consult with a Catholic priest. Susan Stafford brought up a friend, Father Terry Sweeney, who sat with Rock and asked if he wanted his sins forgiven. Rock nodded and accepted communion as well as the anointing of the sick.

On the posts of Rock's bed, Tom began to hang religious medals and images received by fans and friends. "Tell me why not?" he wondered. Martha Raye had handed him a gold medallion that had "gotten me through two tours of Vietnam," and Tom had placed it on the bed.

Clarence carried a fresh bunch of ginger up to Rock's room and set it in a vase on Friday, September 27. "Good night, Rock, keep your faith," Clarence murmured softly. "I'll see you again on Tuesday."

"I doubt you'll see me on Tuesday."

"I'm going to see you."

Clarence brought an orchid from the greenhouse and placed it, floating in water, on Rock's nightstand on Tuesday. "Here's your favorite orchid," Clarence announced. Rock's eyes were open but locked on the ceiling, and he made no response. Clarence couldn't sleep that night. Death is approaching, he reasoned. No, it can't be; I must have misunderstood.

Dean Dittman had been by after church on the weekend. "Rock's out of it," Tom had muttered, but when Dean entered the room, Rock exclaimed, "It's Dean!" Dean noticed a smile that he thought was transcendental--a smile he had seen when Rock was listening to wonderful music or watching a film he cherished. Dean believed Rock was "letting me know he knew something--that he'd learned something from all the pain and anguish he'd had to endure during that devastating year and a half." He was home in his head." Later, Rupert Allan arrived and stated that Rock possessed "an ascetic quality I'd never seen." I thought he was lovely, like a Christ figure."

On Monday, September 30, I requested to see Rock, fearing it would be the last time. His eyes were closed, his naked arms protruded from beneath the covers, and he shivered. Tom leaned forward and said, tenderly, "Are you cold?" Tom drew his blanket up to his chin. Rock's skin was translucent, and he was a fragile skeleton, yet as I stood there, he opened his eyes and smiled with an amazing light. I wondered where it was coming from. His body had reduced to nothing, and all of his brightness was concentrated in his eyes.

Toni Phillips, the night nurse, told Tom the next night, October 1, "I haven't told you this before, but I'm a member of the prayer vigil the Boones have been holding, and they want to come back and pray with Rock."

"Get 'em over," Tom urged.

Pat Boone laid a Bible on Rock's chest and took his hand while he was unconscious. Tom climbed into bed with Rock and cradled him, as Eleanor collapsed on the floor and began speaking in tongues. Pat Boone urged Tom to put out clothing for Rock after the prayers because a miracle would happen in the night and Rock would feel so good in the morning that he would want to get up and dress. Tom went to his closet and put on gray slacks, a blue and white striped shirt, a sport coat, shoes, and socks. "Those will be his happy clothes," Boone declared, instructing the nurse to put them on him first thing in the morning.

On Wednesday, October 2, James was the first person to enter Rock's chamber. There was Rock, laying on the bed with his arms outstretched, fully dressed in his shoes and "happy clothes," which had grown so large that Rock appeared lost inside them. "He was lying there like a doll, not moving at all," James recounts. Because a shift was changing, two nurses arrived and began transferring Rock to a chair, where they raised him upright. According to James, Rock was in pain as they moved him, and clear liquid was dripping from his mouth over his sport coat. When Tom Clark arrived at seven o'clock, James commented, "Mr. Clark, he doesn't look at all comfortable or well."

"Get him undressed," Tom instructed.

Rock seemed to come back to life after he was back in his pajamas and wanted to watch the Today show. James went shopping since the sickroom needed more disinfectant and Rock liked Swiss Miss tapioca puddings. Tom and Rock had coffee, spoke about the news, and at 8:30, Tom stated, "I'm out of coffee." "Would you like some more?"

"No, not right now," Rock replied.

Tom went down to the kitchen, and the nurse buzzed him a few minutes later. "Could you please come upstairs?" When Tom entered Rock's room, he noticed the nurse in tears. "We've already lost him." They reached for each other and hugged, and Tom then requested to be left alone with Rock.

"But I hadn't paid attention because I thought Rock was going to live," Tom explained, "because I thought Rock was going to live." Rock had specified that he wanted to be cremated and his ashes spread at sea, but Tom couldn't recall how the process worked. Mark Miller, ironically, had flown to New York for that one day. Tom called Dr. Kennamer and then went to inform Marc that Christian Rock had died. "Do you want to go see him?" Tom brought Christian into the room--the first time Christian had been let in since Rock had returned from the hospital. Tom attempted to contact Mark Miller in New York but was unsuccessful. He called Wally Sheft, Claire Trevor, and George in the desert at 9:07 a.m. The news of Rock's death was broadcast on the radio around 9:15 a.m.

Tom is still perplexed as to how the story spread so quickly. When Rock died, there were only three people in the house: Tom, the nurse, and Marc Christian. Tom made three phone calls, and the people he spoke with said they would not speak to the press. Tom assumed that the phones had been tapped, but when the phone bill arrived a month later, it revealed that a call had been placed at 9:07 to a hotel in New York where Marvin Mitchelson was staying. It's probable that Christian contacted Mitchelson, who then informed the media.

James arrived home with the groceries shortly after nine o'clock, and when Tom told him Rock had died, he buried his face in his hands. "No, he can't be, and he isn't!" Dr. Kennamer arrived as he headed upstairs to meet Rock. Elizabeth Taylor called to say she was sending security over. "My God, the gates are wide open," Tom exclaimed, hurriedly closing them. The phone lines began to ring.

Stockton Briggle was getting ready to leave for work when he heard the news. He dialed the residence number and reached James, saying, "Tell Tom I'm on my way over." He arrived at 9:50, rang the gatebell, and when it opened, a yellow automobile followed him in. Shirley Boone and Eleanor exited the car, passing Stockton and Tom on their way upstairs to pray. "I was stunned at the impropriety of it-- they were blubbering and carrying on," Stockton says of Eleanor's lying down on the floor and speaking in tongues. It seemed as if a medieval king had died and his body was being chanted over by women."

"There's no one here except James and Tom," Stockton remarked when he contacted his office. Cancel all of my appointments for today." "I'll take care of this," Stockton said, and began answering the phones: "Mr. Hudson's house." Stockton claims he took over because "no one else could do it." I'm a director, and I was in charge of Rock's previous performance. "Do you know what?" He stroked the armrests of his chair. "I feel a great deal of pride and happiness that I was able to do that in his service."

The van from Pierce-Hamrock-Reed Mortuary came at 10:45 and could hardly get through the gates due to the large number of photographers, reporters, and TV crews in the street. They were clinging to the gates, pushing microphones and flashing lights through the bars. Several others began to climb over the gate, prompting Stockton to cry, "Get back, you're on private property, we'll call the cops!"

Stockton saw the van had two windows in the back. Photographers would be able to shoot through the windows, and Tom was adamant that no one take a photograph of the body. Tom stated that he would accompany Rock all the way to the crematory. "I insist that Rock be treated with dignity."

"Get some towels," Stockton instructed. "We'll just cover the windows." The two mortuary workers inquired, "Where's the body?" before putting on masks and gloves to deposit Rock in a body bag.

"Do they really have to do that?" According to Marc Christian.

"No," Dr. Kennamer responded, "but let them, it's easier not to cause a problem."

James took out two of his own towels, which were vividly colored and had diamond patterns on them. "The towels were hideous," Stockton later said. That house is filled with wonderful things, and Rock was leaving with the tackiest towels in the world hung over the windows." When he heard Stockton's description, James was irritated. "They served their purpose," he remarked.

Ross Hunter walked through the gates as Stockton and James were taping the towels to the truck. He had called earlier and said, "Jacque and I are coming, please make sure we get through the gates," but their Rolls-Royce had been obstructed by press vehicles. "Jacque is trapped in the Rolls!" You must find Jacque! He's been snagged in the Rolls!" Ross sobbed. One of the security guards went off to see if he could assist Jacque Mapes.

Stockton dashed back upstairs to Rock's room just as the mortuary guys began to bring Rock out on a gurney. Tom, Marc Christian, James, Dr. Kennamer, and the nurses were close behind. Eleanor and Shirley Boone had vanished. Ross Hunter entered the crimson room and began hyperventilating as the procession approached the landing. "Oh, Rock, Rock... Oh no!" ... Oh, Tom...... Oh my God...."

"It's okay, Ross, it's okay," Tom assured Ross.

They brought Rock out through the garage to the vehicle, hoisted the body inside, and placed a chair beside it for Tom. "I'm going with you," Ross stated as he attempted to enter the van.

"No, no, stay here, I'll take care of it," Tom replied.

They tried to shut the vehicle doors but couldn't since Rock's feet were poking out.

"Get him on his feet!" The men pushed and tugged on the gurney, and just as the doors closed, Ross passed out. "He collapsed like a bloody sponge," James describes. Marc Christian dashed to retrieve a pillow, which was placed under Ross's head by a nurse. Dr. Kennamer gave him a cursory glance and assured him that he would be OK.

"Where's Ross?" Jacque Mapes inquired as he passed through the gates."

"Oh, no! Oh, no!"

"Let's get going," Tom yelled from the back of the van. "It's over a hundred degrees here!" Tom was dressed casually in a blue sport shirt, khaki jeans, and an I LOVE ROCK button. "Don't you want to put on a sports coat?" Stockton said.

"No, Rock doesn't care," Tom responded.

Moshe Alon, Elizabeth Taylor's chief of security, suggested that a backup car follow the van to the crematory. He dispatched a security to retrieve his vehicle, but it took him twenty minutes. Ross Hunter was back on his feet, crying and exclaiming, "He was the best friend I ever had!" as he walked back and forth between the house and the gates where the press had gathered. "Let's get out of here, it's boiling, we're dying!" Tom yelled from inside the van. I couldn't care less about security!"

When the guard returned with his car, the van began to exit the gate. The reporters encircled it and began climbing on the van, prompting Stockton to exclaim, "Don't you people have any decency? "Don't you have any family?"

"I sure hope they don't open the back door," the driver said from inside the van.

"What!" exclaimed Tom.

"You son of a bitch, get off there," Stockton shouted.

"We can't lock it," remarked the driver.

Tom dashed to the door, grabbed the handles, and yanked them shut. He rode on his knees all the way to the crematory, grasping the doors and straddling Rock's body.

The gates were locked when they arrived at the crematory to keep the press out. Rock was placed on a gurney and transported into the facility, where there was a cardboard box labeled ROCK HUDSON. They loaded him into the box, re-loaded it onto the trolley, and rolled it into the oven. "I noticed the package caught fire. "I stood there watching it, then they shut the oven and I left," Tom explains. "It was the most difficult thing I'd ever had to do, but I did it and no photographs were taken."

The next morning, I discovered Tom sitting on the red-tile patio, gazing out over the pool. "There's such a void," he commented. "I put so much effort into making him healthy, and I honestly thought we were going to lick it. Oh, no! I'm disappointed that we didn't." He popped open a can of beer. "I have all this energy, and suddenly I don't have any floors to wash."

Tom took a sip of his beer. "At the very least, I'm relieved that Rock is here in his own bed." He wasn't in discomfort since I brought the dogs in every day. I'm going back to my house today to think about it, then get back to work." Tom went to a twelve-step program for alcoholics within a few weeks following Rock's death and did what he had never been able to do while Rock was alive: stop drinking. According to his friends, he became "a different person; the negative qualities faded, and all the positive things we loved about Tom came to the fore--his humor, charm, warmth, and caring."

On October 20, 1985, thirty-five people gathered in the fog in front of Marina Del Rey's Warehouse Restaurant. They climbed a ladder onto the motor yacht Tasia II while wearing windbreakers and caps and holding bouquets of flowers. When everyone was on board, the yacht set sail for the Catalina Channel, where Rock Hudson's ashes would be spread.

A memorial service and party for three hundred persons had taken place the night before at the Castle. Rock had preferred a party on a yacht with champagne and mariachis rather than a memorial ceremony. But there were too many guests for a yacht, so Rock's inner circle agreed to hold the celebration at the Castle.

Tom was in charge of organizing the last big party at Rock Hudson's residence. Then Elizabeth Taylor intervened, deciding on a Quakerstyle memorial service in which everyone may share their recollections of Rock. She requested pink and white flowers, whilst Tom requested vibrant colors. Tom had requested Mexican finger food-passed, whilst she had requested coffee and a sweet table. She didn't want any writers or public relations people there, even if they were friends of Rock's, and names on the guest list were scratched off and reinstated right up until the wedding.

On the croquet lawn behind the house, a white tent and rows of seats were set up. The ceremony had been scheduled for 5:15 p.m., and Elizabeth Taylor entered wearing a navy and white gown with a long rope of pearls, and the service began.

Constance Towers and John Schuck performed an I Do! I Do! medley. Father Sweeney requested a moment of quiet so that everyone might pray for Rock. Then Elizabeth Taylor onto the stage and recounted the night she and Rock invented chocolate martinis. Other buddies stood up and spoke one by one. Carol Burnett described convincing Rock to do I Do! I Do! as "the most fun I've ever had on a stage." Faye Nuell, who co-produced the show, reported Rock's exclamation, "I got my step!" Stockton Briggle described the "ten-snot scene" in Camelot, while Susan Saint James discussed how Rock celebrated Christmas. Rock's superb instincts as an actor were noted by Roddy McDowall, and his kindness was described by Tab Hunter. Everyone commented on his laughter and how he liked to break people up. Don Morgan, one of Rock's early publicists, recalled the account of when Rock met President John F. Kennedy. "They were seated next to each other at a fund-raising dinner, and President Kennedy had obviously been briefed on the situation." When he sat down, he told Rock, 'We have something in common-we're Irish, and they believe all the Fitzgeralds are linked.' 'Oh?' asked Rock, pausing. 'That will make Ella happy.'"

"Rock would have wanted us to be happy--let's raise a glass to him," Elizabeth Taylor said as she finished the service. People flowed through the house and out onto the patio, where mariachis played and waiters passed out margaritas and little tacos, and there were flowers and paper lights in the trees. As the sun set, the candles and fireplaces were lit, making the house cozy and lovely, with its large sofas and log ceilings. It was a one-of-a-kind environment that transported you back to grand old Spanish days in California. Small groups gathered in the rooms, and everyone agreed that it was a shame Rock's house had to be sold.

Sunday morning, there was not a single individual whose name was a household term or who could be recognized by the two photographers who, despite numerous ploys to keep them away, had managed to turn up at the harbor for the burial at sea. The event had been code-named "George Nader's birthday party," and it was, indeed, George's birthday. The whole Castle staff, Rock's attorney and business manager, four female cousins who had lived with Rock in Grandma Wood's house, a dozen male friends, and three of Rock's lovers: Tom Clark, Marc Christian, and Jack Coates were among the visitors. (Mark Miller had inadvertently neglected to invite Ron Channell.) Mark proposed that the three lovers each hold the container of ashes, but Tom refused. He would be the only one to scatter the ashes.

"By what right does he...?" someone inquired.

"He just does," stated Mark.

On the way out, there was a joyful spirit; everyone laughed and spoke as the boat sailed through the fog to the open sea. The engines were turned off, and everyone assembled on the foredeck. Susan Stafford read the Twenty-third Psalm in the silence, interrupted only by the lapping of waves. The sky was dark, and the lake was a murky green. Tom sat on the prow, holding a brown plastic jar with the words ROCK HUDSON written on the lid. He touched it to his breast, lowered his head, and dropped the contents into the water all at once. The ashes descended like a powdered cloud over the surface and vanished in seconds. We flung flowers, lilies, and carnations, and Tom hurled a maile lei brought by a bunch of Green Berets in Hawaii. The captain began driving the boat in a slow circle around the flowers. They'd been tossed around, but to our surprise, they fanned out and created an almost perfect ring as they bobbled on the water. Everyone leaned over the rail, marveling at the flowers as we sailed in larger circles around them.

On the way back to shore, no one spoke. Dean Dittman held the hand of Jack Coates, who clutched a cluster of miniature white narcissus in his other hand, while John Dobbs cried softly. Mark Miller would later recount how, at the moment the ashes were dumped, a seagull pooped on his blue cashmere sweater. Rock, according to Mark, was "having the last laugh."

The Beverly Crest house continued to operate as if Rock were still alive. There was a frenzy of plotting and strategizing to attempt to avoid a lawsuit by Marc Christian and the ensuing scandal. Susan Stafford visited with Christian, Rupert Allan took him to lunch, and George Nader spoke with him. All of them offered to assist Christian in obtaining the necessary funds and insurance, and Christian told them that he had no intention of suing and had only gone to Mitchelson because he needed a powerful ally. Even as he made these guarantees, papers for the court action were being prepared. The drama was now moving on its own, like a Greek tragedy that, once begun, must be completed until the stage is littered with bodies and everyone is bloodied.

Marvin Mitchelson informed Rock's attorneys that Christian desired a large payout. Wally Sheft instructed James to have the Castle locks changed, to ask Christian for the keys to the Seville, and to deny him cooking rights. On October 25, Christian began moving out, and the next night, James discovered that the playroom had been stripped naked of electronic equipment, films, and records. The Hudson estate would charge Christian in a cross-complaint with stealing three video recorders, nearly 7,000 records, 150 videotapes of films, eight pieces of audio equipment, a computer, a video camera, and Hudson's most elaborate needlepoint rug. He had attempted to steal a large-screen television, but the security chief, Moshe Alon, had yanked it from Christian's station wagon. "Most of the things I took, Rock had given me before I moved into the house," Christian explained. "He told me the records were all mine and said, 'Anything you need, just consider it yours.'" Tom Clark requested that Christian return the records since they were a valuable collection that should be donated to a public institution. "Rock never gave you anything, and you know it."

Christian and Mitchelson held a press conference on November 2 to announce that they were suing Hudson's estate, Mark Miller, Wallace Shen, and two unidentified doctors for $14 million for conspiring to threaten Christian's life. The employees at the Castle witnessed it in the kitchen, and James became pink with wrath. "How dare he dragged Mr. Hudson's name through the mud!"

In a later interview, Christian stated, "I don't care if I win money in court." I made my point; I refused to be treated like an ant or a nonperson."

Mark and George left the desert and took up residence in the Castle to guard it until it was sold. James carried on with his habits, heading to Theodore's in the morning to shop for supplies. Clarence was there every day, pruning and trimming plants, and John Dobbs came in to clean the house.

Clarence was in the kitchen one late November day, making himself a bowl of ice cream. He had arranged sprigs of ginger on the counter, with their gorgeous yellow blossoms that had the most enticing aroma. The ginger had been planted and cultivated by Rock and Clarence, and Rock had always looked forward to the summer when it would bloom. "He was some man, as far as I'm concerned," Clarence replied. "He adored his coworkers." He treated me as if I were another member of the family.,,

"He never paid you very well," one of the employees remarked.

"It makes no difference. It's not so much about the income as it is about who you work for."

Clarence finished his ice cream and took the ginger in his arms, intending to take it up to the room where Rock had slept for the previous twenty-four years. "It was one of his favorite flowers," he remarked.

"How long does it take to bloom?" I inquired.

"From July fifteenth to September fifteenth."

"But..." "But... it's November."

"This is an unusual year." This has never happened before." Clarence's wise eyes twinkled with delight. "I believe Rock's spirit is in the flower." That's how Japanese philosophy works." Clarence calculated how much time had passed since Rock's death. "50 days?" That suggests he's already passed through the first river." Clarence grinned and bowed his head. "He's already on his way to Nirvana."

Printed in Great Britain
by Amazon

31245503R00079